12.00

Elements of Psychopathology

The Mechanisms of Defense

Elements of Psychopathology
The Mechanisms of Defense

Robert B. White, M.D.

Professor of Psychiatry
University of Texas Medical Branch at Galveston
Training and Supervising Analyst
Houston—Galveston Psychoanalytic School
and the New Orleans Psychoanalytic Institute

Robert M. Gilliland, M.D.

Professor of Psychiatry
Baylor College of Medicine
Houston, Texas
Training and Supervising Analyst
Houston—Galveston Psychoanalytic School
and the New Orleans Psychoanalytic Institute

Grune & Stratton

A Subsidiary of Harcourt Brace Jovanovich, Publishers
New York   San Francisco   London

Library of Congress Cataloging in Publication Data
White, Robert Brown, 1921-
    Elements of psychopathology.

    Bibliography: p.
    Includes index.
    1. Defense mechanisms (Psychology) 2. Psychology, Pathological. I. Gilliland, Robert M., joint author. II. Title. [DNLM: 1. Defense mechanisms. 2. Psychopathology. WM100 W586e]
RC454.4.W45   616.8'9'07   75-29072
ISBN 0-8089-0913-4

Grune & Stratton, Inc.
111 Fifth Avenue
New York, New York 10003

Library of Congress Catalog Card Number   75-29072
International Standard Book Number   0-8089-0913-4
Printed in the United States of America

Contents

Foreword

I first came across the mechanisms of defense during my residency training—I thought I had found the touchstone of dynamic psychiatry. Disparate theories and experiences with patients suddenly fell into a semblance of order. My confidence in work with patients increased. But these illuminating insights soon dimmed; the examples turned out to be oversimplifications, had not kept pace with advances in theory, and, on closer study, often proved contradictory. In reading this new book on the mechanisms of defense by Robert White and Robert Gilliland I again experienced the excitement of discovering a key to therapeutic work. Only this time, with repeated readings my enthusiasm continued to grow.

Seldom are the mechanisms of defense given adequate emphasis in psychiatric training. This is regrettable because they are basic elements, the building blocks, of all behavioral disorders. They are not limited to psychopathological conditions, but are of significance in all forms of human interaction and life experience. Thus, all workers in the mental health field should have a thorough knowledge of defense mechanisms. Indeed, such understanding is of value to all who work with people.

To some degree the term psychopathology is a metaphor in that it likens the essential nature of behavioral disorders to structural and functional changes associated with all diseases. When first introduced, the concept of the mechanisms of defense brought a much needed dynamic point of view to the Kraeplinian descriptions of psychiatric disease. With time, these earlier descriptions of these mechanisms came to be viewed as too limiting, much as the earlier principles of physics after which they were modeled. Psychopathology has been passed over as static, descriptive, and lacking in therapeutic relevance. Students tend to slight these fundamentals and rush ahead to the genetic determinants of the behavior disorders, the broader social theories, and the therapeutic encounter.

This state of affairs has occurred for several reasons. The existing descriptions of defense mechanisms often fragment behavior, divorcing it from real life experience. Rather little effort has been made to bridge the gap between defenses and the more complex constellations that comprise clinical syndromes and diagnostic categories. Thus, defenses are not seen as relevant to actual psychiatric practice. The mechanisms of defense have seldom been reexamined in light of expanding theories of Ego psychology, personality development, studies of the family, and the broader social field.

In this book, the authors have taken a giant step that should rectify these deficiencies in training by focusing deserved attention on the mechanisms of defense. Their presentation offers the student the means to gain the fundamental understanding of psychiatric disorders needed to develop skills for rational therapeutic intervention. All of the basic information needed to fully understand the mechanisms of defense is brought together in a most readable form. The presentation goes far beyond the early simplistic descriptions of defense mechanisms, putting them in the full context of current theories of anxiety, instinctual drives, Ego and Superego, and developmental principles including the epigenetic, maturational, and experiential.

Drawing on their extensive knowledge of psychoanalytic theory and rich clinical experience, the authors have presented all of the basic concepts that are necessary for the understanding of psychopathology in the first chapter. Their presentation is clear and concise yet at the same time conveys the full complexity and the profound implications of these fundamental psychological truths.

The descriptions of the defense mechanisms themselves are thoughtfully organized to meet the needs of the student. The beginning examples are relatively simple and easy to comprehend. Gradually the clinical examples are expanded to encompass increasing detail until they ultimately reach a level where each is a clinical vignette. Particularly helpful are the cross references among the examples which serve to demonstrate how frequently multiple defense mechanisms are operative in any piece of behavior.

Although the authors prepared this book with students in mind, their descriptions are of value to a much wider audience. The presentation of each defense mechanism is systematically organized into general comments, definition, clinical examples, clinical syndromes which illustrate the mechanism, and examples of the occurrences of these mechanisms in normal behavior. In short, this format presents the information in a logical and understandable sequence which helps to facilitate the learning process. The book serves as an excellent review as well as a reference for the experienced psychiatrist and psychoanalyst.

The section covering the mental processes of identification, sublimation, and compensation represents a significant advance in the understanding of these complex concepts. Earlier contributions have seldom differentiated clearly between the defensive aspect of these processes and their role in personality development. The authors have clarified both the developmental and the defensive aspects of these processes, and have provided examples of the situations in which they are most likely to serve as a defense mechanism as well as examples of their use in normal development. This allows an easy differentiation between the use of identification, sublimation, or compensation in the service of emotional growth and their use in defensive withdrawal.

The more than one hundred clinical examples serve not only as illustrations for particular defense mechanisms but they introduce the reader to a wide variety of clinical situations. Those drawn from the authors' therapeutic work frequently show how understanding of the defense is utilized in treatment. Case examples bring the theoretical discussions to life because of the broad range of discussion from minor lapses in the normal person to the most severe disturbances, as well as the coverage of a varied spectrum of mental disorders, and clinical settings.

The chapter on defense mechanisms in normal behavior effectively demonstrates how psychiatric disorders are truly on a continuum ranging from severe disturbances to the behavior of the well-adjusted normal person. This chapter is of particular benefit to medical students and physicians outside the field of psychiatry in understanding that the psychiatrically ill are like everyone else, only more so. Of particular interest to the experienced psychiatrist are the discussions of the differential diagnosis of those conditions on the borderline between the normal and pathological.

This book is of value to the non-psychiatric physician in general medical and surgical practice. Understanding of defense mechanisms helps the physician to recognize the psychological overlay encountered in the treatment of the physically-ill person and increases his awareness of how defenses may interfere with accurate diagnosis and impede the establishment of a cooperative alliance with the patient in the treatment of his illness. By the understanding of defense mechanisms the physician will be less threatened and better able to treat all patients.

Sections on symptom formation and the clinical syndrome provide the essential link between defense mechanisms and actual psychiatric entities. They serve as an introduction to more advanced study and work with patients by making the bewildering array of psychiatric symptomatology more comprehensible.

In summary, this book encompasses psychological, psychoanalytic, medical, and social aspects of the topic in an interesting and comprehensive approach. These points of view which sometime appear as competing and antithetical are integrated into a unified system.

June 7, 1975   Robert W. Gibson, M.D.
President-Elect, American Psychiatric Association
Medical Director and Trustee, The
Sheppard and Enoch Pratt Hospital

Preface

There are few sources to which students of behavior can turn for a systematic treatment of the psychological mechanisms of defense, a subject crucial to psychopathology. We have attempted to provide such a source in this book. In doing so we have tried to present the mechanisms of defense and related basic concepts of psychopathology in a form that is concise, simple, and free of undefined psychoanalytic terminology. We have also tried to keep our views consistent with the more sophisticated and complex aspects of psychoanalytic thought which we have omitted from explicit consideration. Because of these omissions some of the concepts we have presented are incomplete, but we trust not incorrect.

We are indebted to numerous people for their help in our efforts. A number of colleagues have provided valuable criticism of the manuscript. We wish to acknowledge our indebtedness and gratitude to the following colleagues at the University of Texas Medical Branch at Galveston: John Bruhn, Harry Davis, Charles Gaston, Harold Goolishian, John Vanderpool, Robert White, Jr., and Stewart Wolf. Colleagues at the Baylor College of Medicine to whom we are similarly indebted are: Gary Byrd, Glenn Cambor, William Cantrell, David Freedman, and Alex Pokorny. We are also indebted to Mary Kuhn of the Yale Child Study Center at New Haven for her helpful criticism of the manuscript and to Joe Tupin of The University of California at Davis. Dr. Tupin participated with us in a series of discussions several years ago; the book stems from those discussions.

Several of our students were exceptionally helpful critics, most notably Peggy Hostetter and Allen Stark at Baylor and Thomas Mareth at the University of Texas. Without the unflagging patience of our wives and the tireless work of Anna Marie Rudd, Louanne Fossler, and Anita Jones, the manuscript would still be in rough draft. Now that it is complete, we hope it will be useful to our readers.

Robert B. White
Robert M. Gilliland

Elements of Psychopathology

The Mechanisms of Defense

1
Basic Concepts

GENERAL COMMENTS

This small book, designed primarily for medical students and beginning graduate students in psychology or psychiatry, is written within the psychoanalytic frame of reference. The numerous other theoretical frames of reference from which the material in this book might be viewed, are mostly omitted to provide a concise treatment of psychopathology and the mechanisms of defense.

To understand the mechanisms of defense, the reader must be familiar with the basic psychoanalytic theory of the structure, function, and development of the psyche—that is, the mind. Consequently, we shall begin with a resume of psychoanalytic theory. Because it stresses those aspects most relevant to psychopathology, our resume presents a one-sided view of the psychology of man: one that depicts childhood as overly fearsome, conscience extremely vindictive, human motives unduly base, and existence largely conflictual. But this is a book on psychopathology, and to balance the view of human psychology presented here, the reader must turn to other sources for psychoanalytic concepts about what is more normal and right in man—such as Erikson (1963), Spitz (1965), Anna Freud (1965), White (1963), and Fraiberg (1959).

CONSCIOUS, UNCONSCIOUS, AND
PRECONSCIOUS MENTAL PROCESSES

Familiarity with the psychoanalytic concepts of conscious, unconscious, and preconscious mental processes is necessary to understand the mechanisms of defense. The difference among these concepts is relative and the three terms indicate varying degrees of accessibility to awareness. The term *conscious* refers to those mental functions (impulses, memories, thoughts, feelings, perceptions) of which the person is aware at a given moment. The term *unconscious* refers to those psychological processes of which the person is unaware and of which he is incapable of becoming aware by any ordinary effort of will. The term *preconscious* refers to mental functions of which the person is unaware at a given moment but of which he can become aware by searching his memory, focusing his attention, or being reminded by someone else. This deliberate effort to become aware of that which is preconscious may succeed immediately, or it may take minutes, hours, or days. Sometimes, it may require the help of others as when a person forgets a name in a social conversation. He may ask others to help him think of the name that he has temporarily forgotten. They may not remember either, but may say, "Wait a minute, it will come to mind." Then the several people deliberately scan their memories but the name may still elude them. Someone may then say, "That name was Dubriski, or Donbriski, or something like that." Others will say, "No, that's not it, but that is close." Then shortly someone will say, "Oh, now I remember, it was Dilbriski." At that moment all will say, "Yes, of course," immediately recognizing the proper word when it was provided. For some reason the name was momentarily not available to consciousness. Usually, a name is excluded in this manner from consciousness by some motivation or wish to prevent it from being conscious. When this is so, often one of the conversationalists may say, "I think I couldn't remember his name because I never liked that guy. He has a sour disposition. But that's how I recalled his name—he is like a pickle but more like a sour pickle than a dill pickle."

At other times various psychological functions are kept preconscious because we must exclude them from awareness to focus attention more sharply on some pressing task or concern. For example, when a person writes an important letter, he excludes from his awareness one or more other pressing issues such as an income tax form that needs to be completed, discomfort from sore muscles caused by too much exercise, or the music from the sound system in the adjoining room. If these other sensations and motivations are allowed into conscious awareness, they distract him from the task at hand. To write the letter most efficiently, the person must exclude from awareness all other pressing motivations, thoughts, memories, and sensations. Sometimes preconscious or unconscious urges that are personally unacceptable become so intense and press so vigorously for expression that they threaten to come into conscious awareness or overt expression whether or not the person wants them to do so. They then become a threat to his ability to control his mind.

DEFINITION OF THE CONCEPT OF MECHANISMS OF DEFENSE

The term *mechanisms of defense* refers to the various automatic, involuntary, and unconsciously instituted psychological activities by which the human being attempts to exclude unacceptable urges or impulses from awareness. By excluding the urge from awareness, he removes it one step further from the likelihood of expression—after all, the thought is said to be the father of the deed.

According to psychoanalytic theory, an urge or impulse is sufficiently unacceptable as to call into play mechanisms of defense when, in the unconscious judgment of the person, its expression would provoke dangerous punishment or retaliation from other people or from that internal judge, conscience. Consequently, when such an impulse presses for expression, the person becomes apprehensive, just as he does in any danger situation.

The assessment of the potential consequences of an impulse is not a conscious and deliberate process. Rather, it is spontaneous, automatic, and takes place outside of awareness. The judgment may be supported by realistic considerations, or it may be based entirely on childlike and irrational views regarding the consequences of the impulse and the anticipated response of others to it. How rational or irrational the judgment is depends on the person's previous life experiences. Any urge that has become correctly or incorrectly associated with the threat of disapproval, punishment, or retaliation will be viewed as dangerous.

One may well ask how a person can form a judgment about the potential consequences of an unconscious impulse without being aware that he is doing so. The answer to this seeming paradox will become clear in later sections. Briefly, the mind monitors its own functions and does so silently and outside of conscious awareness. Speech is an example. As we attempt to express thoughts verbally, the integrating and steering functions of the psyche organize our thoughts and control our tongues in a manner that allows the thoughts to be expressed coherently and in the form that we intended. The intricate feedback mechanisms that make this possible operate outside of conscious awareness.

Although evoked by the need to avoid the threat of impending loss of control over an unacceptable impulse, defense mechanisms may continue to operate even after the original threat has subsided. The defense may then become habitual and firmly entrenched within the person's character structure and usual mode of behavior. A patient who defensively reacted to his own sexual curiosity in childhood by becoming a lifelong public leader in a campaign against pornography illustrates this point.

FEAR AND ANXIETY

The Signal Function of Fear and Anxiety

An adult responds with similar subjective experiences and physiologic changes to either fear or anxiety. Both fear and anxiety are characterized by a subjective sense of apprehension and by physiologic activation of the autonomic nervous system. Both serve as automatic, involuntary signals that alert the person to a serious threat to his well-being. Fear signals the awareness of an external situation that is perceived as an actual, objective danger; anxiety signals an internal psychological danger—an impending loss of control over an unconscious, unacceptable urge.

Fear (unless it turns into panic) sharpens the senses, makes thought precise, and concentrates it solely on the danger at hand, facilitating effective responses to cope with the danger. At the same time, autonomic physiologic changes triggered through the sympathetic nervous system prepare a person for vigorous fight or flight by the outpouring of adrenal hormones and increased blood sugar, pulse rate, respiration, and blood pressure. When fight succeeds, the danger is eliminated; when flight succeeds, the danger is put at a safe distance. Either response lessens the threat and reduces the fear.

Because anxiety signals an inner threat from some impulse or motivation of the person himself, defense by fight or flight is ineffective. Instead of fight or flight actions, anxiety evokes automatic and unwilled psychological mechanisms of defense which attempt to contain and, if possible, so strongly oppose the threatening impulse as to exclude it from awareness. Thus, when successful, either fight –flight responses against an external danger or the mechanisms of defense against an internal psychological threat lessen apprehension. In conversational speech, the terms *fear* and *anxiety* are usually treated as synonyms. Here we use these words as technical terms to distinguish the difference between the signals evoked by threats from two very different sources.

In the course of his evolution, man has developed biologically innate signals that warn him of dangers and prepare him for defense. Fear alerts him to danger from without—some person or situation in the environment that might harm; anxiety alerts him to the inner danger of impending loss of control over an unconscious impulse that threatens painful consequences if acted on.

Physical disease poses an actual threat from within the body. The question arises whether this threat from inside the body is to be considered as an external danger and the apprehension it causes is, therefore, to be considered fear, or whether this is an internal danger, in which case the apprehension should be designated as anxiety, according to the way we have defined terms in the preceding paragraph. The terms *external* and *internal dangers,* as we use them in this book, refer to dangers subjectively perceived as arising within or from outside of one's sense of psychological self. Although the danger caused by physical disease (coronary occlusion, for example) arises inside the body and is in the physical sense an internal danger, it is experienced psychologically as a danger outside of the observing self. It is, therefore, an external danger, psychologically speaking. Indeed, the words people use to describe pain reflect the way they regard the painful body part as being outside of the sense of self. A common expression used to refer to a severe headache is, "My head is killing me," as if the aching head is perceived as an enemy who is attacking the person from outside. Thus, the threat from disease inside the body is treated as identical to any external actual danger. According to our definition of terms, it produces fear rather than anxiety.

The Development of Fear and Anxiety

Fear and anxiety seem to share the same biologic origin and are represented in the neonate's automatic inborn startle reflex in response to loud noises or sudden loss of physical support. We assume that these reactions antedate the infant's capacity to perceive and identify dangers in the environment, potentially dangerous needs and impulses within himself, or the apprehension the infant later experiences when the mother is absent.

Evidence from studies on child development indicates that during the first 6 months of life the infant gradually becomes aware of his own feelings of comfort and discomfort. He cannot yet discriminate clearly among various kinds of discomfort or their sources—discomfort from sources inside him such as hunger, thirst, or emotional need for comforting contact with his mother; or discomfort from sources outside himself such as cold wet diapers, or emotional tension in his mother. Although all of these produce observable discomfort, the infant cannot differentiate unpleasant stimuli arising from within himself from those impinging on him from outside his body. He does not yet realize his diapers are not part of his body or that he and his mother are separate beings. Only as he develops a capacity for organized visual, tactile, and auditory perception and as he accumulates a store of memories does he recognize other people and things as entities separate from himself.

Around the age of 2 to 3 months, the first evidence of organized perception appears in the form of the baby's smiling response to the visual stimulus provided by a human face when it confronts him so that the eyes and nose are visible. This is not yet true social response. The infant smiles as readily at a Halloween mask as at his mother. This innate response is, however, the biological basis for social interaction. It evokes pleasure and loving response from the mother; this in turn pleases the baby and thereby enhances a progressive and mutually satisfying cycle of interaction between them. A satisfactory relation with the mother provides the baby with the foundation for the capacity to form satisfactory relationships with other people later in life.

Between 6 and 8 months of age, the infant's capacity to perceive and remember is sufficiently developed for him to demonstrate apprehension at separation from his mother or the approach of a stranger. Either event is a threat. The absence of the mother disturbs the infant because he has now identified her presence as necessary for his comfort and the alleviation of his needs. The strange face causes apprehension apparently because it clearly contrasts with the reassuring face of the mother and makes the baby aware of her absence. These apprehensions over separation from the mother or the approach of a stranger later differentiate into anxiety and fear respectively. But as yet the infant is unable to identify external dangers and is fearless about such perils as flames, animals, and sharp objects. However, he does begin to sense that when his mother is present he usually feels relief of tension stemming from within (such as hunger) or from without (such as cold wet diapers), and when she is absent, he often experiences painful tension from inner or outer discomforts that cannot be relieved without her care.

The father and other care-providing, familiar people increasingly share the mother's security-producing functions for the infant as he grows older. Even so, in our culture, for the first several years of life the child in distress usually turns to his mother who remains his most important source of security and comfort.

Beginning about age 2, as a result of painful experience and parental teaching, the child progressively learns which external situations constitute a danger. The burned child learns to dread the fire, as the saying goes. But a full and dependable capacity to judge reality correctly and avoid dangerous external situations evolves slowly over the 12 years of chldhood and, in some measure, over the next 10 or more years of adolescence and young adulthood.

The presence of the mother (and later of either parent) protects the child against extreme apprehension and fear of external dangers —even when the parents can give no real protection from the danger. Anna Freud and Dorothy Burlingham (1943) observed this in the behavior of children in London during the blitz of that city in World War II. In the presence of sturdy parents who did not panic, children suffered relatively little apprehension from the noise and danger of exploding bombs. On the other hand, when separated from their parents and sent to rural child care centers safe from bombs, the children suffered great apprehension as a consequence of the separation itself, a greater threat for children than the danger from bombs.

By the age of 3 years the child has begun to develop some judgment and foresight concerning external dangers and has begun to learn that he must control his own impulses or suffer pain of parental punishment or disapproval. He progressively develops apprehension about the external dangers in the real world and about loss of control over impulses from within—especially sexual and aggressive impulses. At the age of about 2½ years, an assertive youngster may seriously injure another child as they quarrel in the sandbox for possession of a shovel. He may bloody his adversary's head with no compunction and then turn to using his shovel on the sand. By the age of 6, having been repeatedly scolded (even ever so gently) for overtly expressing such impulses, the child ordinarily has internalized the reprimanding voice of parents as the voice of his own conscience and is able to feel guilt. He now scolds and reprimands himself for doing—even just for wanting to do—something that conflicts with his childish sense of morality. Thus, between the ages of 3 and 6 years the child develops the ability to feel apprehension over inner impulses as well as outer dangers, and gradually acquires a stable, enduring, and predictable internal system of self-regulation: the Ego and Superego.

Loss of control over unacceptable urges creates apprehension on several scores. Such impulses are primitive and infantile. Their overt expression might result in punishment, for example, a parental scolding for the hostile aggression of the child in the sandbox. However, some anxiety stems not only from the dread of punishment but also from the dread of helplessness that occurs when one loses control over his impulses. In the adult, impending loss of control over strong, unacceptable impulses creates a vague dread of helplessness and total psychic disintegration which is experienced as a fear of "going all to pieces" or "exploding" or "coming apart at the seams." This threat of catastrophic helplessness revives childhood fears of being overwhelmed by strong impulses as in a violent temper tantrum, or by intense needs experienced during the total desolation of loneliness when the mother is absent.

When the threat comes from an inner impulse, fight or flight, so effective against external dangers, fail. To cope with such internal threats, man has evolved psychological maneuvers to keep an unacceptable impulse (and the feelings and ideas associated with it) out of awareness. The mechanisms of defense serve to exclude an unacceptable impulse from consciousness, thereby diminishing the threat psychologically. Unacceptable impulses that are kept outside of awareness and under secure control no longer threaten and consequently no longer provoke anxiety. Excluding a threatening impulse from awareness does not lessen or destroy the impulse. Although unconscious, it remains active and intact. Efforts to contain it must continue, much as guards must continue to keep a dangerous criminal in jail once he has been arrested and removed from society by the court. In adults, the keystone mechanism of defense for exercising such containment is repression, most of the others being auxiliary defenses called into action when a repressed impulse threatens to come into conscious awareness.

THE INSTINCTUAL DRIVES OF THE ID AND THE NATURE OF THREATENING IMPULSES

The term *Id* refers to the constellation of unconscious motivations stemming from the primitive sexual and aggressive instinctual drives, and in conjunction with the terms *Ego* and *Superego* comprises the components of the so-called structural theory of the mind. The concepts Id, Ego, and Superego are useful abstractions that describe and categorize certain important motivational and organizing functions of the mind. They are not to be viewed as actual neurophysiologic entities with measurable or identifiable anatomic locations.

Instinctual drive in human beings refers to an innate, biologically determined urge to action. The exact pattern of behavior that such an urge prompts is not inborn; it is highly dependent on learning, and varies from person to person according to his life experiences. The protean expressions of human sexual and aggressive behavior clearly reflect this.

Primitive instinctual drives are expressed with relative openness in the behavior of small children and persist in less obvious form in the behavior of the adult. From time to time, everyone consciously experiences an aggressive or sexual impulse that must be denied expression or suppressed (that is, deliberately put out of mind), because such expression is not condoned by the real life situation or the person's conscience. For the most part, such conscious components of sexual and aggressive drives are relatively adult feelings which do not trigger anxiety since they are under secure control and are not unduly primitive or infantile. In addition to these relatively mature urges, man is motivated by components of instinctual drives that are unconscious and primitive. These primitive and ordinarily unconscious urges produce distress if they break into awareness, even if they are not overtly expressed. They do so because they revive the primitive fears of punishment or retaliation that accompany childhood conflict over sexual and aggressive impulses, and because they also conflict with the adult's moral values and his judgment about their realistic consequences.

In childhood, conflict over impulses that are at odds with the conscience produces both guilt and also fear of the external danger of parental punishment and disapproval. Children tend to imagine that parental punishment will be violent, destructive, and based on the talion principle of an "eye for an eye." The child's irrational fear of punishment will be described further in the section on Superego formation. In adults, anxiety stemming from unconscious infantile impulses may revive this childish dread of harsh and vindictive punishment by others, especially others in positions of authority. Consequently, when earlier conflicts are revived in the adult, he tends in a childish way to feel that he cannot tolerate disapproval from others because it will be so harsh as to endanger, perhaps even annihilate him. Thus, both subjective, irrational anxiety and objective fear ultimately signal a potential external danger.

The real dangers that may result from the unbridled expression of primitive and infantile urges were tragically illustrated by a man who went on a wild rampage of murder during a total mental breakdown. His traumatic childhood resulted in a frail and vulnerable central controlling agency, his Ego and Superego. His control was further impaired by disordered brain function (toxicity from amphetamine abuse and fatigue from an extended period of sleeplessness). His psychological integration was additionally disturbed by difficulties in his current relationships with friends. His controls collapsed. Primitive and destructive aggression broke through as he began to shoot at anyone he could see from the roof of a tall building, wounding and killing numerous people. His rampage ended as police stormed the roof and shot him down. His impulses indeed provoked talion punishment and the ultimate danger—annihilation.

THE LIFE-NECESSARY BIOLOGIC NEEDS

The term *instinct,* as ordinarily used in biology, must be differentiated from the term *instinctual drive,* as used in psychoanalysis.

Instinct refers to an inborn, unlearned pattern of behavior that is triggered by specific external stimuli. The seasonal migration of some North American birds is an example. When the days get shorter, the nights longer, and the temperature cooler, these conditions trigger the instinctive behavioral pattern of flight southward to warmer climates.

A related category of human motivations is the life-necessary instincts: the needs for air, water, food, and elimination of waste products. These needs give rise to inborn patterns of behavior that are relatively independent of experience. For example, variations in the style of eating do occur, but these are superficial differences in form dictated by custom and etiquette. Men from any culture eat in almost identical ways when they are starving.

In technologically sophisticated societies the life-necessary needs are of relatively little significance to psychopathology. They assume great psychopathologic importance if they become entangled with sexual and aggressive drives, as in psychogenic obesity. In this syndrome the biologic need for food becomes intertwined with infantile emotional needs for security and love. A person with this disorder eats voraciously and at times defiantly, not to fulfill nutritional needs but rather to feel loved and comforted. Food has become a symbolic substitute for love and security. Such a symbolic meaning for food stems from the infantile experience of nursing during which the baby so indiscriminately equates food and being fed with love and security.

Two characteristics distinguish the life-necessary needs from the sexual and aggressive drives. First, life-necessary needs can be satisfied only by highly specific substances. If a person is thirsty, no liquid will do but water; if he is hungry, no substance will do but digestible and nutritional food. The need to breathe can be satisfied only by oxygen. In contrast, the sexual and aggressive drives are highly displaceable and can be more or less satisfied in a variety of ways. A sexual urge, for example, can be gratified to some degree through fetishism, fantasy, or highly sublimated activity that has little apparent sexual connotation. An aggressive urge felt toward one person can be partially discharged toward an entirely different person or inanimate object as when a man, angry at his boss, later berates his wife or smashes a lamp. The second distinguishing characteristic of the life-necessary instincts is that the person dies if they go unsatisfied for even a short time, whereas sexual and aggressive urges can go ungratified indefinitely without jeopardizing life.

CONTROLLING, STEERING FUNCTIONS OF THE
PSYCHE: THE EGO AND THE SUPEREGO

The Ego, Its Development and Functions

The term *Ego* refers to the constellation of functions that comprise man's controlling, steering, and coordinating psychological agency. This agency gives form, order, and precision to adult behavior in contrast to the diffuse, random, and poorly organized behavior of small infants. The Ego provides the adult with the ability to perceive realistically, remember accurately, think logically, act skillfully, and foresee consequences correctly—in short, it is the Ego that organizes behavior to be realistic and mature rather than childish, impulsive, or wishful. This technical meaning of the term Ego is quite different from its popular meaning which tends to equate it with egotism ("He has a big ego."), self-esteem ("It was good for his ego."), or selfish self-interest ("He is on an ego trip.").

The Ego begins to develop in the early weeks of life, reaching its highest degree of organization in mature adulthood. It evolves in accordance with the epigenetic principle. Governed by that principle, development stems from the interplay of two factors: the maturation of biologically innate tendencies and learning through experience.

The Epigenetic Principle of Development

The development of the embryo proceeds in accordance with the epigenetic principle; that is, it develops from a stage of minimal anatomic and functional differentiation to a state of maximal differentiation and complexity, and does so in a fixed, biologically innate sequence and at a genetically predetermined rate. Beginning as a clump of essentially identical cells, parts of the embryo differentiate and selectively grow at various appointed critical periods of time as the different organ systems evolve into a coordinated whole that enables the infant to survive independently outside of the mother's body.

In this stepwise process of organization and differentiation of cells, each organ system has its developmentally critical time period. Each organ must arise at its appointed time—no sooner, no later —if it is to develop fully and be properly coordinated with other organs that arise earlier, concomitantly, or later. For example, if a limb bud does not arise within its critical time period, it will be forever stunted, distorted, or skewed in its form, function, and its relation to other organ systems with which it must be properly integrated if the total organism is to become a viable, balanced, and properly organized whole.

The earlier in development that a suppressing or distorting influence is imposed on a growing part of the fetus, the more severe will be the resulting stunting or distortion of its final form and the more extreme will be its lack of integration with other parts of the fetus. Thus, when one organ system misses its critical moment, its relationship with other closely coordinated organ systems will be disturbed. Hence, the frequency of multiple congenital anomalies in defective fetuses. At birth the infant is still developing physically. The nervous system in particular has almost two decades of postnatal development before it is anatomically and physiologically complete and optimally organized.

Erik Erikson describes how the epigenetic principle applies to postnatal psychological development just as it does to prenatal physical development. First the mother, and later both of the parents, the family, and the wider society provide the organizing influences that mold personality development just as DNA and RNA guided the prenatal physical development of the child. In this regard, Erikson (1959) states: "The healthy child, given a reasonable amount of guidance (by loving parents who are reasonably at peace with each other), can be trusted to obey inner laws of development, laws which create a *succession of potentialities for significant interaction* with those who tend him." Further: "Personality . . . (develops) according to steps predetermined in the human organism's readiness to be driven toward, to be aware of, and to interact with, a widening social radius, beginning with the dim image of a mother and ending with mankind. . . ."

The application of the epigenetic principle to psychoanalytic concepts of personality development highlights three important issues:

1. The earlier in life that disturbing influences impinge on the organism, the more widespread and pervasive will be the impairment or distortions of development.
2. Each stage of personality development, like those of embryological development, involves phase specific critical time peri-

ods for each particular budding psychological attribute. Each particular capacity must be met by adequate environmental conditions if it is to emerge at its appointed time; otherwise it will remain forever stunted or distorted to some degree.

3. Unless the unfolding of new attributes at each stage is satisfactorily completed, growth of succeeding attributes at later stages is jeopardized; impairment at stage 1 prejudices development at stage 2; impairment of both stages 1 and 2 imposes still further handicaps for development at stage 3, and so on. In this fashion, early faults in development may lead to an ever-greater accrual of psychological vulnerabilities. Conversely, early successes foster an accrual of psychological competence. Later, of course, more healthful influences may compensate for earlier deficiencies.

Psychoanalytic concepts of personality development emphasize that for genetically sound children (and this includes the vast majority), the crucial factor determining personality development is the quality of parental care and family organization, especially the quality of maternal care in the first year or two of life.

Maturational Factors in Ego Development

Such Ego functions as perception, consciousness, vocalization, and motility are present in primitive form at birth. They do not depend on experience or learning for their appearance. Other basic functions such as the ability to sit up, stand, crawl, walk, and control the bladder and bowel sphincters depend very little on learning in the usual sense, but their emergence greatly depends on the physical and emotional stimulation the normally affectionate and mature mother automatically gives her baby as she holds, fondles, feeds, and cares for him. If provided such emotional nurturance, these Ego functions appear at predictable times during the infant's first 2 years of life, even if no one attempts to teach them to him. Infants deprived of such emotionally nurturant stimuli fail to develop optimally no matter how well fed and clothed. The same applies to the development of organized visual, auditory, or tactile perception. Without emotional nurturance, these sensory functions will not mature adequately.

At birth the infant has only one identifiable behavior pattern that is totally independent of experience and that also involves his clear ability to respond to a specific stimulus and exhibit a highly organized motor action. If the newborn infant is hungry enough to be alert, but not so hungry as to be wailing in agitation, he responds to a gentle stroke on one cheek by turning his head to that side and making sucking movements with his mouth. If the other cheek is stroked, he turns his head to that side as he sucks. If the upper and lower lips are touched simultaneously, he suddenly stops turning his head, fixes his head and neck, and then makes a snapping movement of his mouth, sucking even more vigorously. If the nipple or any other object is present to be grasped by his lips, he sucks on it. This configuration of organized perceptual ability and coordinated motor skill has high survival value, allowing the infant to meet the mother halfway as she attempts to feed him.

For several weeks it appears that the newborn infant cannot attach any meaning to what he sees, hears, or feels. For many months, he apparently has little or no capacity for memory, attention, or thought. Unless loved, he will fail to develop meaningful responses to what his senses tell him, and his ability to focus his attention, to think, or to remember will be basically disturbed. Consequently, he will be unable to grow into an adequately responsive social being, and will, to some degree, remain psychologically an infant. Such an arrest of development is referred to as a *fixation*. When fixation (discussed in Chapter 6) occurs at an infantile stage, it results in the person's remaining self-centered and uncaring about people or things around him except as objects to meet his immediate needs. It also leaves the person more vulnerable to regression when he encounters stress in later years (a topic we shall also discuss in Chapter 6).

Love and security are essential also for the development of those more complex Ego functions such as thought, speech, judgment, or the capacity to tolerate frustration and delay gratification of need, although learning through instruction becomes of greater importance in the development of these more complex functions.

Experiential Factors in Ego Development
(Learning)

Those Ego functions that are more clearly dependent on experience and learning for their development include such higher intellectual functions as the ability to read, to write, and to do arithmetic. Their acquisition depends on stimulation from experience as well as on the maturation of the nervous system. Although learning in its more usual sense of mastery through systematic teaching is of crucial importance, inadequate emotional nurturance for the child will seriously impair his capacity to learn these higher skills, no matter how well they are taught. But long before the child is ready to master these higher order skills that require effort to learn and someone to teach, other more basic functions must develop: functions present at birth only as inborn potentials.

The capacity to remember and to pay attention to specific things and people as well as the capacity to defer personal needs and wishes must first appear before the child can concentrate his efforts on mastering new and difficult skills. Definite evidence of the capacity for attention and memory appear between the second and sixth months when the infant begins to recognize and respond expectantly to the human face and the feeding situation. This indicates that he is learning to attach meaning to what he perceives and he is developing the ability to focus his attention on people and objects and to remember them. In this same period motor control gradually improves and around the age of 6 months he begins to grasp objects intentionally and move them about as he wishes—which mostly means putting them in his mouth.

Between the ages of 6 months and 24 months other important Ego functions evolve. The infant demonstrates a progressively greater ability to wait for what he wants, to tolerate frustration and delay. He develops an increasing sense of security that allows him to tolerate the mother's absence with less distress. And, of course, speech and motor skills such as walking and some degree of sphincter control also appear.

The development of these abilities depends above all else on the experience of security in the infant's relationship with his mother. If he can construct in his memory a mental representation of his mother as a dependable person who is sure to be present most of the time when he needs her, he can afford to become sufficiently autonomous to develop control over his own body and emotions and to be independent of her. Only the mental representation of such a dependable mother can comfort and reassure him when she is not in his immediate presence, and endow him with a sense of trust that she has not disappeared forever.

Piaget's studies on cognitive development, so admirably summarized by Elkind (1970), support psychoanalytic observations that under the age of 18 months children are unable to be certain that either things or people exist if they are not within sight or hearing.

Thus, when the mother is away, the infant is unable to feel secure in his knowledge that she, in fact, still exists. Only the development of an internalized mental image of mother sustains him in her absence and gives assurance of her existence. Unless he gradually develops such a dependable inner mother, the infant suffers some impairment of almost all Ego functions. If he is severely deprived of experiences that build such an inner source of security and trust, basic Ego functions such as the ability to walk, to talk, to learn, to think, to remember, or to trust himself or others will be distorted or stunted. Later, the child's capacity to cope with the more disciplined demands of learning social and intellectual skills will be impaired; his tolerance for frustration will be poor; his control over impulses and feelings will be undependable; and his ability to form affectionate, trusting, and caring relations with others will suffer.

In the infant's second year of life, familiar people such as the father, grandparents, siblings, and others become additional sources of comfort and security. Even so, as Spitz (1965) and others have shown, the loss of the mother for even a few days during the period between 6 months and 24 months of age may profoundly disturb the psychological functions of the infant. Interference with development or loss of already attained abilities will be generally proportionate to the length of her absence. Long absences may produce severe extended or even permanent disturbances; short absences, temporary and milder disturbances.

The Basic Functions of the Ego

The major component functions that make up the coordinating, steering agency we designate as the Ego are

1. Perception
2. Consciousness
3. Memory
4. Attention
5. Thought
6. Intelligence
7. Speech and language
8. Motility and motor skills
9. Judgment and foresight
10. Capacity for the delay of needs and impulses
11. Mechanisms of defense
12. Signal affects: anxiety, depression, shame, and guilt

The various Ego functions and the coordination among them usually operate silently, effortlessly, and outside of conscious awareness. For example, as previously noted, speech ordinarily requires no conscious effort. In casual conversation, the speaker usually has no awareness of what words he will use next in his sentence. He relies on the silent and unconscious capacity of his Ego to supply the appropriate word to complete his sentence so that his verbal expression of thought is coherent, lucid, and to the point. If unexpectedly called on to speak publicly on a question of major importance, he speaks very deliberately and chooses words with conscious effort to be sure that he says what he intends, mentally rehearsing his utterances before saying them aloud. Fatigue, intoxication, lesions of the brain, or psychological conflict interfere with the silent and ordinarily reliable integrative functions of his Ego, and may cause him to utter words he did not intend to say. A slip of the tongue results, or he says things which are inappropriate or which he "didn't really mean."

The Ego operates somewhat like a computer. Through our perceptual equipment we take in data from our environment and data from our inner impulses, feelings, and desires. These multiple data are integrated so that we behave in a manner that most adequately satisfies (1) our inner motivations, (2) our moral standards, and (3) the demands of reality. A crucial function of the Ego, then, is to arbitrate the best possible bargain among these contending and, at times, contradictory sources of motivation.

Signal Affects: Anxiety, Depression, Guilt, and Shame

The Ego is the psychological agency that perceives and attaches meaning to inner and outer stimuli, and it organizes, directs, and coordinates behavior prompted by such stimuli so that it is most advantageous to the person. Early in infancy, affects or feeling states are the automatic experiences that arise in the infant when needs which are strong enough to enter awareness are frustrated. Still helpless to take action to alleviate needs when they become intense, the small child experiences them as unpleasant feeling states and endures them until they are met by the mother. Pleasurable feelings automatically occur when needs are met by her. Unpleasant feeling states can only be signaled to her by his motor agitation and wailing. As his own Ego functions develop and he becomes increasingly able to take effective action on his own, feeling states associated with the build up of strong needs gradually become useful as signals that prompt him to take action. Hunger, a feeling state originally passively endured by the child until the mother fed him, now prompts him to seek her out and ask for food, or in later childhood, to find food for himself.

The affect of *anxiety* is assumed to be the original feeling state experienced when intense needs become so urgent that a state of painful, helpless tension develops. Gradually, fear, signaling a threat from an external danger, becomes distinguished from anxiety which signals a threat from an internal danger. Although anxiety is conceptualized as the primary motive for defense, and the one which calls into play the unconscious defense mechanisms of the Ego, there are other familiar unpleasant feeling states against which the person attempts to defend himself by any means available. For the most part, these other feeling states (which are also experienced by the Ego) are mostly determined by the Superego. They include depression, shame, and guilt, unpleasant feelings with which we are all familiar.

Depression becomes the affect that signals actual or anticipated loss of love and approval. Around age 3 to 6 years, when the Superego is becoming a dependable inner psychological agency, the affects of guilt and shame become established. *Guilt* signals the threat of self-disapproval for acting or intending to act in ways at odds with the moral standards of the Superego—of being deemed bad and unworthy by one's own moral standards. *Shame,* closely related to guilt, signals the danger of being judged as foolish or inadequate in the eyes of others and of being ridiculed by them—or of appearing foolish in the eyes of oneself as when one feels "ashamed of himself." Thus, when the sensing functions of the Ego signal an impending loss of control over unconscious impulses, anxiety is experienced. When fantasied or real loss of love and approval is sensed as a consequence of such loss of control of unconscious impulses, depression is the signal. When impending self-accusations of badness are sensed, guilt is the signal. When the threat of humiliation and ridicule is sensed, shame is the signal.

The Ego may sense such impending threats before the dangerous impulse or urge is translated into action or even before it enters awareness. When that occurs, signal affects evoke Ego defenses to lessen the threat. In response to such signals, the mechanisms of defense are silently instituted. The person concerned is unaware that defenses are being called into play and has no knowledge of their purpose.

The Superego, Its Development and Function

In addition to the Ego, the other internal psychological agency that modifies and controls man's behavior is his Superego, often equated with conscience. In adulthood, conscience is composed of internal moral values that are relatively enduring and independent of external circumstance. This configuration of controls directs man to behave with moral consistency even in the absence of other people, the force of law, or other social standards of behavior. The totality of these conscious and unconscious moral steering and controlling functions, in conjunction with man's ideals and aspirations, is designated as the *Superego.*

Like the Ego, the Superego usually operates silently, automatically, and unconsciously. We become aware of its presence and function only when guilt signals conflict between intentions or actions and the standards of the Superego, or when a sense of exuberant self-satisfaction signals that motives or actions are judged especially praiseworthy by the standards of the Superego.

The forces of the Superego have an unconscious component that is primitive, infantile, and absolute. This aspect of the adult Superego is the residual of the inflexible and punitive morality characteristic of early childhood. It hearkens back to the period from age 3 to 6 years when the Superego is being organized and the inner voice of conscience is becoming an enduring internal guardian of behavior. Psychoanalytic studies of childhood and Piaget's study of cognitive development in children show that at this age the child's thought is characterized by animism, egocentricity, literalness, and omnipotence.

Animism refers to the tendency to endow all objects, animate and inanimate, with feelings, motivations, and the power to act. When the small child falls from a hobby horse, he spanks it and calls it "bad," believing the horse deliberately hurt him.

Egocentricity refers to the child's tendency to assume everyone else thinks, feels, and perceives the world as he does. When an angry 3-year-old does not want to be seen, he covers his eyes and assumes that since he cannot see others, they cannot see him.

Literalness refers to the child's tendency to give concrete interpretations to words and actions. When he is told by an angry parent that a God who knows his every thought also watches his every move and will punish him by sending him to hell if he misbehaves, the child envisions God as a real person who always watches and knows even his most secret thoughts, and who may at any moment physically snatch him away to hell. A less ominous example of the literal interpretation which a child gives to the comments of adults is the instance of a 5-year-old who heard his mother say facetiously to a friend that the new house they were building was going to be "the world's most expensive greenhouse." By this joking comment the mother referred to the great expense of the house because of its design which allowed plants to be grown in the living room. A few days later, the bricks for the new house arrived. On seeing brown bricks being delivered, the alarmed child immediately ran to tell his mother that the bricks were the wrong color. They were brown and the house was supposed to be green!

Omnipotence, the child's inability to distinguish between a thought he has harbored and a deed he has actually performed, is most evident around highly emotional wishes. His envious wish, often explicitly stated, that a new sibling should be taken back to the hospital and left there may haunt him dreadfully if the new baby becomes ill and has to return to the hospital. He feels he has caused the baby's illness. If the baby dies, the older child may be left with the dread that he is a murderer.

The child's imagination flourishes at this age and his mental images are vivid. His capacity to discriminate between thoughts and real events and to understand cause–effect relations is so poorly organized that he easily and thoroughly misunderstands many things. He begins to understand death as a state in which people (or animals) close their eyes and do not respond to noise or touch. Since he knows sleeping people do this, the child frequently confuses death with sleep, a confusion reflected in the childhood prayer, "Now I lay me down to sleep. I pray the Lord my soul to keep. If I should die before I wake, I pray the Lord my soul to take."

Confusion stemming from his literal thinking causes many events considered insignificant by adults to be profoundly important to the child. A child who is told by an exasperated parent, "You will be the death of me," interprets these words with absolute literalness. He believes himself capable of killing his mother or his father with naughty thoughts or behavior.

Sometimes adults make cheerful comments intended to please the child and are perplexed when their words cause apprehension rather than joy. Fraiberg (1959) provides a delightful example of this in the case of the little boy who could not fly. David, a precocious child age 2 years and 6 months, was delighted at the prospect of a trip to Europe with his parents. They told him of the wonders of such a trip and how mother, father, and David would all fly to Europe 2 weeks hence. As the day of the great flight approached, David became moody and depressed. His parents became concerned and tried to find the cause of the youngster's uncharacteristic moodiness. Finally, David tearfully confessed the cause of his distress: "I can't go with you because I don't know how to fly!"

The ensuing discussion between David and his parents made clear the cause of David's despair—he did not know how to fly. He assumed his parents did, and consequently envisioned the day of departure as one on which his parents and he would go outside on the lawn, flap their arms like birds, and fly off to Europe. But David knew that he had not yet learned to fly, though he assumed his parents could. His tears stemmed from his vision of himself deserted and alone as his parents flapped off into the sky and headed for Europe, leaving him on the ground, alone and disconsolate.

Egocentrism and animism in the child's thought compounds his difficulty. He believes anything that moves or has physical effects on him lives and feels just as he does; consequently, chance occurrences and actions are imbued with remarkable meanings. If something pleasurable happens, it is because people or things like him. When something unpleasurable happens, it is because people or things dislike him. For example, if a child is scolded because his curiosity prompted him to stick his finger into a light socket, the child feels angry and hurt. If he resumes his explorations and receives a painful shock, he believes the socket intentionally hurt him because he has done something bad. If the parent further responds to his screams of distress with a distraught, "I told you that you would be hurt if you disobeyed Mommie and put your finger in there again," then the child may be convinced that Mommie and the socket have colluded deliberately to punish him for disobedience. If the mother adds, "You can be killed by doing that," the consequences of disobedience assume even more terrifying proportions in the child's mind.

Since the ability to control strong feelings is still poorly developed, the child may well physically hurt his mother in a moment of anger. When she responds with a sharply worded, "Stop that, you're hurting Mommie," his anger becomes endowed with the power to hurt. As yet incapable of clearly distinguishing between the reality of a thought and a deed, the child equates angry thoughts and wishes to hurt with the fearsome actuality of inflicting real harm. This fantasied ability to harm the parents is even more frightening because the child also loves them and realizes how desperately he needs them. Such is the awesome way the preschool child experiences his world.

Still other characteristics of the child's view of the world increase his problems in this period between age 3 and 6. First, he is physically small and weak in comparison to his parents. He egocentrically assumes that they have the same feelings and impulses that he does and that they are as incapable of controlling such feelings as he often is. His wish to inflict hurt during moments of anger may then provoke fears that the parents have identical and equally uncontrollable wishes toward him. Because he realizes the parents are so much larger and more powerful than he, the consequences of the uncontrollable rage he attributes to them appears potentially deadly. With parents who indeed are childlike and unable to control their impulses, we see the actual parental expression of such deadly childlike rage in the battered child syndrome.

Another characteristic of the child at this age concerns his biologically innate tendency to develop a rivalry with the parent of the same sex and an erotically toned attachment to the parent of the opposite sex—the Oedipal relationship discussed more fully in the section on Identification (p. 97). Sexual play, curiosity, and imagination flower at this time. The jealousy-ridden triangle the child constructs in his relation with his mother and father is fraught with anxiety and fear of physical retaliation. Realizing the hopelessness of his rivalry, the child normally resolves his dilemma by abandoning the erotic aspect of his attachment to the parent of the opposite sex and by relinquishing his rivalry with the parent of the same sex by identifying with him, and adopting the philosophy, "If you can't beat them, join them." This identification, a process of becoming like the parent, helps to consolidate the internal moral controls (Superego) of the child and his basic sense of sexual identity.

When the inevitable tendencies of the child to misunderstand events coincide with a continuous reinforcement from strongly held parental attitudes, the effect on the child's personality development is even greater. If the home atmosphere is warm, fair, and one of firm but gentle discipline, it promotes optimal growth and the formation of a reasonable conscience. But even under such ideal circumstances, the animism, egocentricity, literalness, and omnipotence that is characteristic of the child's thought inevitably makes his conscience to some degree unreasonable, vindictive, and arbitrary. When the home atmosphere is punitive and harsh, it fosters the development of a conscience that is implacable in its demands for perfection. For example, if a child reared by very strict parents is caught in normal and innocent sex play, he may be warned never to repeat such bad behavior and told that God will know if he does and will send him to hell forever. Should the remainder of his rearing repeatedly reinforce such inflexible morality, then the childhood layers of his conscience will condemn any sexual curiosity or activities with any person under any circumstances as being bad, forbidden, and dangerous. In adult life, his conscience may then forbid socially appropriate sexual impulses, and impotence or frigidity may result. The unconscious aspect of his Superego adheres to the absolute injunction received in childhood that he must "Never do such a thing! Ever again!" Conversely, a child reared by exceedingly indulgent parents may become an opportunistic and self-indulgent adult, incapable of exercising adequate moral controls or self-discipline.

By age 6, conscience has become an enduring internal controlling agency. But since it is absolute and rigid in childhood, no matter how fair or reasonable the parental discipline, the Superego must later undergo revision and modification if it is to be workable in adulthood. The adolescent usually rebels against the tyranny of his rigid infantile conscience, and, as a consequence of this rebellion the Superego is reorganized in a more mature and realistic form. Adult conscience tends to be less absolute, vindictive, and arbitrary; it is more flexible, relativistic, and capable of distinguishing shades of gray between the black of bad and the white of good. Nonetheless, every adult harbors unconscious vestiges of the rigidity and inflexibility of the Superego of his childhood. These psychoanalytic conceptualizations of Superego formation are also supported by data from the direct observation of children which Piaget (1948) first described in 1932 in his book *The Moral Judgment of the Child.*

THE EXTERNAL WORLD: REALITY

So far we have considered only the Id, Ego, and Superego as the determinants of man's behavior. Stimuli from the environment also affect behavior and may either support psychological integration or help to create psychological conflict. From the point of view of psychodynamics, social stimuli are more important than physical stimuli are, especially since technology has enabled man to achieve reasonable mastery over the physical aspects of his environment. In affluent industrialized societies, most people are not overly concerned with obtaining heat, shelter, or clothes to protect themselves physically from the elements, or with procuring food, water, and air to assuage life-necessary biologic needs. Our technology provides security against physical need.

On the other hand, custom, tradition, mores, laws, and the more personalized expectations of people who are important to us greatly influence behavior and often stimulate psychological conflict. These social influences mold our behavior by inhibiting or promoting the discharge of sexual and aggressive drives of the Id, by reinforcing or weakening moral controls from the Superego, and by supporting or impairing the steering, coordinating functions of the Ego.

Man's eternal struggle to control his sexual and aggressive drives is reflected in the great emphasis on "Thou shall not" contained in two of our oldest codifications of morality, the Ten Commandments and the Hippocratic Oath. Other social codes and customs relax the controls of the Ego and Superego and promote the open expression of otherwise relatively forbidden impulses. During Mardi Gras, for instance, the ordinary rules of conduct are largely suspended for several days. The person is encouraged to turn himself over to the spirit of the carnival, a time of merrymaking that generally involves considerable drinking and free, playful expressions of sexually toned impulses. Usual social and individual standards governing behavior are relaxed for the specific ceremonial period. The greatest revelry occurs on Mardi Gras Day which is immediately followed by Lent, a period of penance and self-denial.

New Year's Eve is another ceremonial occasion which encourages the expression of relatively forbidden impulses. Ordinarily taboo activities such as heavy drinking and kissing strangers often become the order of the evening. On the following day, the merrymakers traditionally enter a period of self-discipline as they commit themselves for the coming year to resolutions of "good" behavior which is usually characterized by self-denial and nongratification of some aspect of instinctual drives.

Another social condition that favors the unleashing of primitive urges is the spirit of a lynch mob which drives its members to behave in cruel, murderous fashion that most of them could never exhibit if acting alone. The unfortunate behavior of many members of an American military unit at My Lai in Vietnam illustrates this phenomenon. Encouraged by the behavior of a few leaders, a number of otherwise honorable soldiers, swept along by a mob frenzy, shot women, children, and even infants.

These examples demonstrate the interplay among the instinctual forces of the Id, steering functions of the Ego, moral controls of the Superego, and social stimuli from external reality. Continuous input of social and physical stimuli is necessary to maintain adequate Ego functions. This has been demonstrated by sensory deprivation experiments in which a subject is placed in a soundproof, totally darkened room and required to lie still or float quietly in water so as to minimize tactile and proprioceptive stimuli. After an hour or less, the subject develops an almost irresistible hunger for sensory input that impels him to resort to self-stimulation by speaking, touching himself, or moving about. In time he usually suffers mounting apprehension because his thoughts become confused, and he may begin to experience hallucinations and delusions. As he progressively becomes unable to think logically or to trust his own senses, he tends to develop a fear of psychological disorganization and insanity. Few people can comfortably tolerate such sensory deprivation for more than a few hours. Some subjects suffer delusions and mental confusion for hours or even days after the experiment, and a few become grossly psychotic and remain so for days or weeks. Thus, in the absence of sensory stimuli, basic Ego functions, such as thought and perception, become disorganized in a way similar to the disorganization seen in severe psychoses and toxic delirium. Deprivation of social stimuli—for example, the extreme monotony and social isolation of solitary confinement in prisons—similarly disturbs the integrity of Ego functions, even under conditions in which ordinary physical stimuli (sound, touch, vision, etc.) are not withdrawn.

On the other hand, excessive sensory or social stimulation can overburden the capacity of the Ego to process and adjust to incoming stimuli. Continuous bombardment with high levels of sound and light produce fatigue and eventually mental confusion. Few adults can long tolerate the jarring of their senses by a rock concert with a light show. Many adolescents thrive on such intense sensory stimulation because such high levels of sensory input distract them from the disturbing inner conflicts that characterize that period of personality development.

Too much stimulation from rapid change in social circumstances also overtaxes the Ego's adaptive capacity. The studies of Holmes (1973) and others have shown that *any* life event which necessitates change and readjustment imposes stress. Too many changes in too short a period of time may overburden adaptive capacities and increase the probability of physical or mental breakdown. For example, Holmes has found that patients with such varied conditions as coronary occlusion, tuberculosis, illegitimate pregnancy, or mental illness regularly show a greater accumulation of stressful changes in their lives during the year or two prior to their difficulty than matched controls do.

Another factor that affects the integrity of the psyche is the physical state of the organism. Physiological disturbances of the brain impair the very organ of the mind. Depending on the site of the disturbance, brain disease may affect the steering, controlling, and coordinating mechanisms of the Ego and Superego, allowing otherwise forbidden Id impulses to gain overt expression. We see this in the crudely sexual and aggressive outbursts characteristic of many patients with organic brain disease. Similar eruptions of forbidden or unwanted behavior tend to occur in persons suffering from toxicity, fatigue, malnutrition, debilitating illness, or hormonal imbalance (such as that which occurs at adolescence or the climacteric).

**DIAGRAMMATIC REPRESENTATION
OF THE PSYCHE**

A pictorial representation of the components and organization of the psyche may be helpful in summing up the various concepts discussed thus far. Schematic diagrams do violence to reality and can represent the complexities of the human mind only in a highly over-simplified manner. But the over-simplification inherent in such schema may give the reader a useful way to review the concepts presented thus far and to summarize them in a manageable fashion.

The psyche can be diagrammed in a way similar to the classic model of the reflex arc. Inner and outer stimuli enter the central steering and coordinating structures of the Ego and Superego. The stimuli are processed, organized, and given form and direction by the Ego and Superego as they emerge as behavior. These basic concepts about the psyche are represented in Fig. 1–1, the first and most highly simplified of our schematic diagrams.

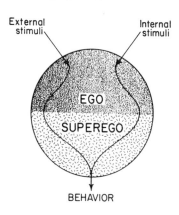

Fig. 1-1. The two types of stimuli (external and internal) which impinge upon the central steering and coordinating functions of the psyche, the Ego and Superego. These agencies then integrate these stimuli in such a manner as to bring about a behavioral response which is most advantageous to the person.

Figure 1-2 is more complex. It specifies the various types of internal and external stimuli and includes the three categories of behavioral activity: thought, motor action, and autonomic discharge. It shows the feedback circuits of the Ego and Superego, and it specifies the other component of the psyche, the Id. The external stimuli are of two types: physical and social. Social pressures and expectations are the forces most relevant to psychopathology. The inner biological stimuli are of two general categories: the life-necessary needs and the instinctual drives of sex and aggression. Those aspects of sexual and aggressive drives that are *unconscious, primitive,* and *infantile* are designated as the Id.

Both Ego and Superego functions have conscious and preconscious components in addition to the major unconscious components. The meaning attributed to a given external stimulus will depend on how the judging and evaluating functions of the Ego and

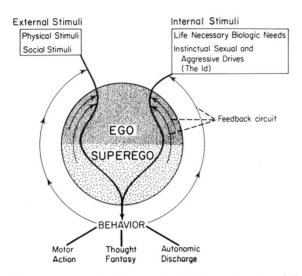

Fig. 1-2. The two types of external stimuli (physical and social) and the two types of internal stimuli (life necessary biologic needs and the sexual and aggressive drives of the Id)—important motivations of behavior. Also illustrated are the feedback circuits of the Ego and the Superego and the feedback effects of overt behavior, which are involved in coordinating and integrating behavior, and the three forms in which behavior may occur: motor action, thought and fantasy, and autonomic discharge. The Ego and the Superego integrate all of the determinants of behavior into a form which best meets the demands of external reality, gratifies biological drives, and conforms to the moral precepts of the Superego.

Superego treat the stimulus. The same applies to stimuli from the internal biological sources. This type of psychological processing of stimuli we represent as arrows indicating a feedback circuit from the memory, the judging, and the evaluating functions of Ego and Superego as they influence the functions of perception, consciousness, and attention. There are, of course, many more such internal feedback systems in the Ego and Superego. But the complexity of the mind is beyond our ability to represent in a schematic diagram.

In addition there are feedback circuits involving the effect of behavior on both external stimuli and internal stimuli. For example, the internal need of hunger prompts the act of eating which diminishes the hunger need.

Behavior may be in the form of (1) overt motor activity, (2) thought (which can be considered trial behavior, rehearsed mentally before being allowed motor expression), or (3) discharge of impulses through the autonomic nervous system (with or without conscious awareness). The latter behavioral response (autonomic discharge) is the basis of the lie detector test and is an important factor in the cause of certain psychosomatic diseases. For example, angry people show an increased blood pressure. This autonomic response may occur even when the person has no conscious awareness of his anger. If this sympathetic activation persists because of chronic unconscious rage, hypertension may result (see p. 42).

In summary, as shown in Fig. 1-2, the Ego integrates external and internal stimuli into a coherent pattern of behavior that best meets the demands of external reality, gratifies biologic instinctual drives, and conforms to the moral precepts of the Superego. Behavior also alters external reality and internal biological drives.

Figure 1-3 represents the mother-infant interaction so crucial in the early development of the Ego. Born almost totally helpless, man requires a longer period of dependence on parental care than any other animal. He needs almost two decades of such dependence in order to survive physically and develop into a psychologically and socially competent adult.

In early infancy, he is as tightly tied psychologically to the mother as he was tied physiologically to her before birth. Prenatally, in addition to her uterus, she lent him the use of her lungs, kidneys, heart, and digestive system. Postnatally, she places her Ego and Superego functions at his disposal as she uses her perception, memory, intelligence, judgment, motor skills, and other of her more highly developed psychological abilities to do those things for the infant that he is unable to do for himself.

Wailing and uncoordinated thrashing movement, the only behavior by which the infant can express his needs, is an urgent signal of distress. That signal has a uniquely compelling effect on the normal mother. It brings her to the infant's side. She then uses her judgment to determine his needs and what skills are required to alleviate them. If she has the sensitivity to judge his needs correctly and the capability to meet them adequately, the baby relaxes and dozes back into somnolence in which he spends much of his time early in life. This cycle of interaction between mother and infant is repeated innumerable times before the child develops sufficient organization and coordination of his own Ego functions to be independent enough of the mother to survive without her constant care.

This mother-infant interaction is represented schematically in Fig. 1-3.

For the mother to respond adequately to the needs of the infant, at least most of the time, two conditions must be met. First, the mother must be reasonably mature, well-integrated, and at peace with herself. The second condition is that she and her infant must be adequately supported by the context of a family that is reasonably at peace with itself and well-supported by the wider society.

She cannot respond sensitively to the needs of her infant if she is too distracted by childish impulses of her own, if she is too harassed by an overly strict Superego or too little controlled morally by an overly lenient Superego, or if she is too lacking in such Ego functions as judgment and ability to tolerate the inevitable frustrations which occur because she frequently must place the needs of the infant ahead of her own. A husband who is too childish to tolerate sharing his mate's affection and time with the baby, or a

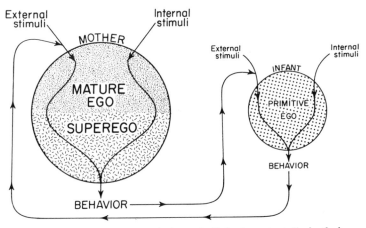

Fig. 1-3. The infant and mother intimately linked postnatally in their psychological interaction as they were linked prenatally in their physiologic interaction. Possessing only a primitive Ego, the infant's behavior is poorly differentiated, and he can express his states of intense need only by wailing agitation. He must depend on the more mature Ego and Superego functions of the mother to sense the causes of his agitation and to alleviate them. No stimuli affect a mother as powerfully as her infant's behavior. When he is distressed, she is compelled to come to his assistance; when he smiles and responds lovingly to her, she is delighted. These cycles of interaction are crucial determinants of the psychological development of the infant.

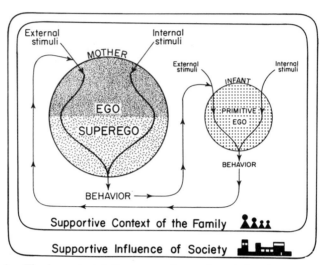

Fig. 1-4.   The important influence on the mother=infant interaction of the
family and of the society in which the family exists. Unless the family
members are reasonably at peace among themselves, the mother=infant
relationship will be disturbed. The family members cannot be at peace
among themselves unless the family unit is adequately supported by the
society at large.

wider society that frustrates the legitimate needs of the family, can
impinge on the mother-infant dyad in ways that impair the caretak-
ing abilities of the mother. This impairment, in turn, disturbs or
distorts the psychological development of the infant. Conversely, a
husband who enjoys sharing the responsibilities of parenthood sup-
ports and enhances the mother in her care of the child and contrib-
utes greatly to the baby's emotional growth. Thus, we may add to
our schematic representation these additional features of the supportive context of the family and the supportive context of the wider
society. As Fig. 1-4 suggests, the family and the wider society hold
and mold the infant even though he nestles mostly in the arms of his
mother.

THE NATURE OF PSYCHOLOGICAL CONFLICT

Anxiety signals an impending breakdown of the controlling,
coordinating functions of the Ego and the threat that unacceptable

Id impulses might come into conscious awareness or overt expression. To be sure, the thought of doing something unacceptable is not the same as the deed. But, as we have noted earlier, thought is father of the deed and the more primitive aspects of the evaluative functions of the Ego, strongly influenced by the more primitive levels of the Superego, may equate thought and deed as does the Biblical dictum, "Whosoever looketh on a woman to lust after her hath committed adultery with her already in his heart."

The moralistic and punitive unconscious aspects of the infantile residues in the Superego treat the unacceptable thought and wrongful deed as equally evil and prescribe punishment for either in much the same retaliatory spirit as the Biblical injunction, "If thy right eye offend thee, pluck it out."

Thus, sexual or aggressive impulses that most people judge acceptable and proper by ordinary social standards may be treated by the primitive and moralistic aspects of the Superego as if they are evil, horrible, dangerous, and deserving of some vindictive punishment. Consequently, the Ego may refuse expression to such relatively harmless impulses in thought or overt behavior. Thus dammed up, such impulses increase in intensity for want of discharge and begin to press urgently, even violently, for expression, in turn evoking from the Ego ever more urgent opposition to the expression of the impulse. In this fashion, the growing pressure of impulses reaches a level of intensity that threatens to overwhelm all defensive efforts. Anxiety signals this threat.

Other conditions that impair the capacity to control unconscious forbidden impulses are as follows:

1. A biologically determined upsurge of instinctual drives (such as sexuality during puberty)
2. External events or situations that stir the promptings of the Id or encourage the relaxation of Ego and Superego controls (such as Mardi Gras, riots, lynchings)
3. External situations that impair Ego controls by fostering regression on a purely psychological basis (such as experimentally imposed sensory deprivation or other extreme environmental stress)
4. Physiologic factors that weaken controls by impairing brain function (such as alcohol, fatigue, senility, etc.)
5. Faults and defects in the organization of Ego or Superego, de-

fects caused by inadequate emotional nurturance during the formative years of childhood

In summary, anxiety may result when Ego controls are impaired physiologically, when impulses are heightened biologically; when social or physical environmental circumstances impair Ego or Superego functions, or stir otherwise well-controlled impulses to clamor for expression, or both; when a rigid and punitive conscience refuses expression of legitimate, socially acceptable impulses and creates a state of being dammed up; or when there are Ego weaknesses resulting from faulty development.

When anxiety is evoked, the automatic, involuntary, and unconscious mechanisms of defense are called into play. When the defenses are successful, anxiety is lessened or avoided altogether.

REFERENCES

Elkind D: Children and Adolescents. New York, Oxford Univ. Press, 1970
Erikson EH: Identity and the life cycle, Psychological Issues, monogr. 1. New York, International Universities, 1959
Erikson EH: Childhood and Society (ed 2). New York, Norton, 1963
Fraiberg SH: The Magic Years. New York, Scribner's, 1959
Freud A: Normality and Pathology in Childhood. New York: International Universities, 1965
Freud A, Burlingham D: War and Children. New York, International Universities, 1943
Holmes TH, Masuda M: Life change and illness susceptibility, in Scott JP, Senay EC (eds): Separation and Depression. Washington, D.C., Amer Assoc Adv Sci, 1973
Piaget J: The Moral Judgment of the Child. Glencoe, Ill., Free Press, 1948
Spitz RA: The First Year of Life. New York, International Universities, 1965
White RW: Ego and reality in psychoanalytic theory. Psychological Issues, monogr. 11. New York, International Universities, 1963

2
The Mechanisms of Defense

There is no universal list of mechanisms of defense, and various textbooks differ in those listed. Despite this variability, a number of defense mechanisms are routinely included in most of the standard textbooks. We shall discuss those mechanisms generally agreed on in the literature and generally included by such recognized sources as Anna Freud (1946), Frazier and Carr (1964), Freedman and Kaplan (1967), Brenner (1973) and Kolb (1973). These mechanisms are

1. Repression
2. Conversion
3. Inhibition
4. Displacement
5. Rationalization
6. Reaction formation
7. Undoing
8. Isolation of affect
9. Regression
10. Denial
11. Projection
12. Turning against the self
13. Dissociation

Three other reactions (identification, sublimation, and compensation) are discussed in Chapter 3. They are sometimes used as psychological defenses, but they differ significantly from the other defenses in that they are also important components of normal development and nonconflictual psychological functioning.

In this chapter, the 13 mechanisms which are exclusively defenses are discussed in sections devoted to each. These sections are organized under the following headings:

General Comments on That Particular Mechanism
A Formal Definition of the Mechanism
Clinical Examples of the Mechanism
Clinical Syndromes Which Illustrate the Mechanism
Occurrence of That Mechanism in Normal Behavior

The reader should keep in mind that the use of these mechanisms is not limited to pathological states. Normal people have unconscious impulses which are primitive, infantile, and incompatible with reality, the judgment of the Ego, or the moral values of the Superego. When these impulses press for expression, the Ego uses defense mechanisms to keep them from conscious awareness or overt expression for normal behavior to continue relatively undisturbed.

REPRESSION

General Comments

Repression is generally considered the basic or keystone defense mechanism used by adults and older children, all other defense mechanisms being auxiliary processes called into play to maintain defense against unacceptable impulses when repression begins to fail. Although the mechanism of denial (see p. 78) blots out awareness of the significance of some unbearable aspect of the external world, repression excludes from consciousness some unbearable inner impulse or some thought, fantasy, emotion, or memory associated with it.

When repression is successful, the impulses that repression defends against are completely banished from awareness. When that occurs, there is no conscious sense of conflict or manifest symptoms. However, the psychological energy expended to maintain repression is no longer available for other purposes. Furthermore, the energies involved in the impulses that have been repressed are also unavailable for use. This results in a limitation of the person's range of behavior or interests. For example, if a person is in conflict over a specific set of sexual impulses and successfully represses them, he may also repress many other related erotic urges. To an observer, such a person will appear to have little or no interest in sexuality; that is, there will be a notable lack in his psychological makeup. The person himself will not be distressed by this—he simply will feel no interest in or inclination toward sexual activity. The constriction of his sexual interest may be the only visible evidence of the operation of the mechanisms of repression.

As we shall discuss in greater detail in Chapter 6 on symptom formation, manifest symptoms occur only when repression begins to fail. Other mechanisms are then called into play: conversion, displacement, or undoing, for example. The result is the formation of a symptom which is a compromise between the impulse and the defense. In part, the symptom helps to maintain defense against conscious awareness or overt expression of the forbidden unconscious impulse; in part, it expresses the forbidden impulse, but in a symbolic form which is sufficiently disguised to prevent recognition of its nature.

Definition

Repression refers to the automatic and unconsciously instituted process through which anxiety provoking urges and associated thoughts, fantasies, feelings, or memories are excluded from awareness.

Clinical Examples

Example 1.   A patient's father was shot to death by a burglar when the patient was only 7 years old. Although this occurred in his presence, he later had no memory of the event, and indeed he had no memory of any experience prior to the age of 10. Frequently, such a very traumatic experience causes all temporally associated events that antedate or follow the disturbing occurrence to be drawn behind the curtain of amnesia. This guards against the recall of any memory associated with the specific traumatic event. Banning these related memories or ideas from awareness is analogous to jailing criminal suspects for guilt by association.

In this example, the question arises as to which of the patient's impulses was defended against by his amnesia. Generally speaking, even an event as traumatic as the murder of one's father, distressing as it would be, does not produce amnesia unless the event is related to a disturbing instinctual impulse. This was so in the case of the boy. Therapy revealed that he hated his father and wished him dead. The murder fulfilled his wish. Amnesia resulted from the need to avoid recognizing his hateful wish.

Example 2. A childish and frigid woman dressed and behaved seductively, but was completely unaware of the erotic aspect of her behavior. She was repeatedly bewildered by frequent advances which men made to her, and was unable to understand why such things happened. Because of repression, she was unaware that her demeanor was sexually provocative or that she unconsciously wished to invite sexual overtures. Instead, she convinced herself that the advances occurred because all men were crude beasts interested only in sex. Thus she resorted to rationalization as an additional defense (*see* Rationalization, p. 56).

Example 3. A 24-year-old businessman sought treatment because he always felt lonely, and for years had sensed that all of his personal relationships were shallow and empty. He had achieved remarkable financial success, took pleasure in a variety of hobbies, socialized easily and extensively, but felt a sense of "incompleteness." He began his psychoanalytic treatment with the comment, "I want you to understand that my problem is not a sexual one—in fact, I have no interest in it whatsoever." Having no interest in sex, he felt that it created neither problems nor pleasure for him. As his treatment revealed, he had no interest in sex because he had successfully repressed his erotic urges. However, the repression of his sexual interest made it impossible for him to form or maintain any close relationships, resulting in his sense of loneliness and incompleteness.

Example 4. A 35-year-old man who was exclusively homosexual had been in analysis for 30 months when he arranged his first date with a female. He was exceedingly conscientious about punctuality, and invariably felt guilty if he did not meet obligations exactly on time. For several days prior to the date, he was intensely preoccupied with it, and talked about it incessantly in his analytic sessions in an effort to prepare himself for this important new experience. On the evening the date was to occur he found himself walking in the downtown area of the city, greatly preoccupied with the thought that there was something he needed to do or needed to remember. As he turned a corner, he unaccountably collided with the side of a building and struck his forehead sharply, sustaining a large and painful bruise. For a few minutes thereafter, he could not understand his carelessness and "stupidity." Then it suddenly dawned on him that this had been the evening for his date, for which he was now 2 hours late. The anxiety-provoking date had been repressed and totally excluded from his awareness. In its place there was only the nagging thought that there was something he had "forgotten." The blow to his head punished him for violating his extremely rigid standards regarding punctuality. Having thus done penance, he was able to "remember" or de-repress the incurred obligation. He also now had an excuse to avoid keeping the date—his headache was too severe.

Clinical Syndromes Which Illustrate Repression

Clinical syndromes or life circumstances in which repression may be observed are

1. Amnesia
2. Symptomatic forgetting (as the man who forgot his date)
3. Slips of the tongue or pen, in which the correct word is not allowed access to awareness or expression
4. Anxiety attacks in which the person feels apprehension but is unable to determine what causes it

Occurrence of Repression in Normal Behavior

Ordinary lapses of memory in essentially normal people demonstrate repression. For instance, a young man forgot an appointment with a prospective employer whom he greatly disliked and feared because of the man's ill temper. It had not occurred to the young man that the prospective employer bore a remarkable resemblance to his tyrannical father whom he hated. Unconsciously, he had sensed that his rage toward his father might erupt in the course of the appointment with the employer. To ensure successful repression of the rage, the threatening business appointment was also excluded from awareness, another example of remanding some thought or urge to the unconscious because of guilt by association. He succeeded in keeping his rage under control but at the price of failing to obtain the job.

In this instance we can see that the young man had an area of conflict of possibly neurotic proportions which motivated his forgetting. If he regularly experienced some disturbance of psychological function in dealing with older men in authority, whether or not they were particularly ill-tempered, he clearly would have a clinically manifest psychological disturbance. On the other hand, if his forgetting of the appointment was a relatively isolated event, this transient disturbance would qualify as an example of what in 1901 Freud (1960) called the psychopathology of everyday life.

Occasionally, everyone experiences some brief disruption of psychological function because of repression. Ordinary lapses of memory, as when one is unable to remember a name, are examples of temporary and relatively normal repression. In those circumstances, the person struggles to recall a name, commenting, "Wait a moment, it's right on the tip of my tongue." If someone else says, "Wasn't the name Morris?," the forgetful person immediately says, "Yes, of course, that's it—I knew it all along, but I just couldn't make it come to mind for a moment." In this instance the name was preconscious, that is, outside of immediate awareness but capable of being brought into awareness by directing attention to it. In contrast, a word or event that is unconscious is incapable of being made conscious by such ordinary mental activity.

Even such ordinary lapses of memory are usually motivated by a wish not to remember. For example, a few years ago a colleague was talking to an old friend, Cyrus, at a psychiatric convention. As they chatted, other acquaintances passed by and he introduced them to Cyrus. After a time, Cyrus teased him about knowing so many people and jokingly commented, "You act like a politician running for office because you shake hands with so many people." The friend's comment irritated him a bit. When yet another friend walked by and he began an introduction, he found he could not remember Cyrus's last name! Embarrassing as the moment was, he had avenged himself on Cyrus. At the moment of his inability to remember, however, he had no conscious awareness that he was getting even. All he sensed was a painful and embarrassing inability to remember the name of a good friend whom he had known quite well for a long time. Such genuinely involuntary forgetting may blend into deliberate and willful action. If one has a social engagement that he does not want to attend, he is more likely to forget it than one he looks forward to. In other instances, one may at the last moment say, "I don't think I will go—I will phone and say I am not feeling well." Here, a deliberate lie, innocent though it may be, is used to avoid an unpleasant situation; being both conscious and willed, it is not a mechanism of defense.

CONVERSION

General Comments

When repression fails to defend successfully against a forbidden impulse, one or more additional mechanisms of defense may be called into play. When conversion is called into play, the impulse is allowed partial expression but in the disguised, symbolic form of some disturbance of physical function. Thus, the impulse is permitted some degree of expression while, at the same time, its true nature is excluded from conscious awareness. For example, a primitive murderous impulse which takes the form of the wish to choke another person to death may be symbolically expressed and also defended against in the conversion reaction of a paralysis of the hands in which the hands are frozen in the clutching position. The clutching posture expresses the intent to choke; the paralysis prevents the intent from being actually carried out or consciously recognized.

Conversion symptoms may include sensory disturbances such as anesthesias, pain, hyperesthesias, deafness, or blindness; motor disturbances such as paralysis, weakness, incoordination, or involuntary movements such as convulsions and tics. Conversion also includes those psychosomatic disturbances which are a symbolic expression of underlying conflict, for example, some types of impotence, asthma, headaches, or digestive disturbances.

However, we wish to emphasize that there are other psychosomatic illnesses (termed *psychophysiologic disorders* in the current nomenclature) which do not represent a symbolic expression of the struggle between an unconscious impulse and the defensive operations of the Ego. These symptoms are emotional in origin but represent only the innate physiologic concomitants of emotional stress. For example, many people turn pale, sweat, and develop rapid heartbeat and diarrhea when they are either frightened or anxious from any cause. Psychologically speaking, these psychosomatic symptoms indicate anxiety and symbolize nothing.

Stewart Wolf (1975) has cited a fascinating Russian experiment that exemplifies psychosomatic disturbances caused by physiologic changes that are innate concomitants of the emotion of anger. In this experiment, a female baboon was separated from her mate and placed in an adjacent cage within his full view. A strange male was then put in her cage. As the female gradually became amorous with this new male, her former mate became agitated and helplessly enraged at the proceedings in the adjacent cage, and in time became severely hypertensive. All of the male baboons who were cuckolded in this fashion developed high blood pressure.

Definition

Conversion refers to the automatic and involuntary process through which a repressed, forbidden urge is simultaneously kept out of awareness and also expressed in the disguised and symbolic form of some disturbance of body function, usually a disturbance of either the sensory or voluntary motor systems.

Clinical Examples

Example 1. A 27-year-old married woman developed abdominal pains which were so severe that exploratory abdominal surgery was performed. No significant pathology was identified at surgery. The pain persisted. The woman was a very intelligent, attractive, conscientious, and ambitious person who had worked diligently to finance her husband's college education. She continued to work as a secretary after his graduation. Lacking drive and ambition, the husband did not advance in his work or his earning capacity, to his wife's great disappointment. In this context, the patient was drawn into the role of referee in a stressful marital triangle involving her very pretty younger sister who had begun an affair with the patient's handsome boss. The patient was soon besieged with frantic inquiries about her boss from her sister, on the one hand, and the boss's jealous wife, on the other. At that point, her abdominal pain began, and she had to quit working.

On careful inquiry, the patient gave a most unusual description of her pain. She stated that it began in her upper thighs and "slithers up into my abdomen—it moves like fingers inside of me—like hot, burning fingers moving in and out." This very moral and religiously devout woman was totally oblivious to the obvious symbolic sexual significance of the "hot fingers" that were "slithering" up her leg and into her abdomen.

Therapy confirmed that the torrid office romance for which she was the referee had increased her dissatisfactions, sexual and otherwise, with her husband, and had stirred temptations to do as her sister was doing. Such sexual temptations were completely at odds with her strict morals. The conflict that resulted was defended against by the conversion reaction which she developed. The pain punished her for her forbidden sexual urges. It also made it necessary for her to stop working; consequently, it removed her from the arena of the turbulent office romance, thus lessening her temptation to engage in a similar affair. The sensation of "hot fingers" slithering up her thigh and into her abdomen also symbolized the gratification of her unconscious forbidden sexual wishes.

Example 2. A man who harbored a great unconscious rage toward men in authority received a mild head injury when a box fell from a conveyor belt at the factory where he worked. At this time he had been very angry at his boss. This anger had even earlier roots in a childish rage toward his tyrannical and sadistic father. When taken to the dispensary following his injury, he felt the plant doctor was not as sympathetic as he should be. Shortly afterward, he developed a staggering gait, headaches, partial loss of sensation over his head, and partial blindness. His symptoms persisted for months and improved only after his vindictive anger toward his boss and the company physician had been assuaged by their attentiveness and a moderately lucrative cash settlement from a lawsuit.

Example 3. A 35-year-old devout Catholic woman was advised by her family physician and her priest to have a tubal ligation because two of her three living children had suffered from severe jaundice in their neonatal period. The jaundice was due to a severe Rh problem in the mother. She was advised that further pregnancies carried a grave risk to the child. She had the tubal ligation, but some months later a routine gynecological examination showed her to be pregnant. The pregnancy was a very difficult and harrowing experience. The patient spent many weeks in the hospital having placental exchange transfusions of blood in an effort to save the child. The child was born alive but moderately jaundiced. Several days after the delivery, the patient was told that on the next day she could at last see the baby and feed it herself, and that she and the baby would be ready to leave the hospital in a few more days. That night she was awakened by a terrifying nightmare—a dream of seeing her baby mutilated and dead. She awakened from the dream very frightened, and immediately got out of bed to seek the assistance of the nurse. Within a few seconds she became completely blind. As a consequence of her blindness she was unable to see the baby the next day, and the plan to discharge her and the baby within a few days had to be canceled. With the help of psychotherapy she slowly regained her eyesight as she gradually became aware of her wish not to have the baby and her great anger at her husband and at the physician who had performed the faulty tubal ligation. Here, we see an example of the eruption into consciousness of a hostile wish to be rid of the baby as the nightmare portrayed. What she had "seen" in her dream was intolerable to her because it was so completely at odds with her conscious feelings of love for her new baby and her very strict and moralistic conscience. Her hysterical blindness symbolically expressed both the wish not to see her baby and the wish not to see the anger in herself.

Example 4.   A 44-year-old man came to his analytic session with severe conjunctivitis of both eyes. He reported that he had just consulted an ophthalmologist who found no sign of infection or trauma and suggested that the patient might be allergic. The patient had awakened that morning with severe burning and itching of his eyes; when he looked in the bathroom mirror, he saw that his eyes were extremely bloodshot.

During the course of his analytic session he reported the following event: The evening before, while watching one of his favorite television shows, he had moved the television set so that he could view it more comfortably from an easy chair. In doing so he had broken the antenna lead at its connection to the antenna, which was situated on the roof just above the room in which he was watching television. Since he had easy access to it from the porch outside his room, he climbed on the roof to make a simple repair. From this vantage point he happened to look into an upper bedroom of the adjacent house, where by chance he saw the adolescent daughter of his neighbor admiring her nude figure in the mirror. She began to fondle her breasts and genitalia, and the patient became so intensely aroused sexually that he felt compelled to masturbate while perched precariously on the roof. On ejaculation, he was overwhelmed by a profound sense of guilt because he realized that the young woman reminded him of his own teenage daughter. In addition, he feared quite unrealistically that his wife might have detected him in his shameful act. He quickly abandoned the antenna project, retreated to his bedroom, and fell asleep. He awoke with bloodshot, itching eyes.

The analyst interpreted the patient's symptoms as an expression of conflict and guilt over his sexual arousal at the sight of the young girl who reminded him of his daughter, and his conjunctivitis disappeared before he arrived for his next analytic session. The patient's need to exclude the significance of this behavior from awareness, in conjunction with the conflict and guilt over his voyeuristic impulse, had been translated into a disturbance of somatic innervation which resulted in the dilatation of the blood vessels of his eyes. A psychological conflict had thus been "converted" into a physical symptom which revealed both the lustful intent of his eyes and in some degree the moralistic injunction, "If thy eye offends thee, pluck it out."

Clinical Syndromes Which Illustrate Conversion

The defense of conversion is most prominent in hysterical neuroses, but it may also occur at times in other psychopathological states. The clinical syndromes or life circumstances in which conversion may be observed are

1. Psychogenic disturbances of voluntary motor functions such as paralysis, tics, and seizures

2. Psychogenic disturbances of sensory functions such as anesthesias, paresthesias, blindness, deafness, and pain
3. Those psychogenic disturbances of respiration, circulation,
   digestion, and elimination which constitute a symbolic expression of both a disowned impulse and the defense against it, in
   contrast to those psychosomatic disorders which result from
   nonspecific manifestations of anxiety or emotional stress

Occurrence of Conversion in Normal Behavior

Although a clear-cut conversion reaction always reflects significant psychological conflict, the defense mechanism of conversion
occurs in psychologically healthy people when they are exposed to
some extreme external stress such as severe civilian disaster or
wartime experience. Small children may exhibit symptoms which
border on conversion reactions when they are faced with some unpleasant situation. For example, the stomach ache of the child who
does not want to go to school.

Another example of conversion in a relatively normal person is
the previously healthy mother who was stricken by a severe, disabling headache a few hours after her 6-year-old daughter was
struck down and killed by an automobile in front of their home. The
car was driven by the daughter of a neighbor who was an arrogant,
wealthy, unpopular man with considerable political influence. Because of his influence, the on-the-spot investigation of the accident
was a travesty of police work.

As the mother of the victim began to emerge from a shocklike
state an hour or two following the senseless death of her daughter,
she developed a severe, disabling, blinding headache. The pain excluded all other feelings, and she showed no signs of grief. Analge-
sics were of no avail. Her physician was called. As she talked to
him, she suddenly poured out a barrage of pent-up feelings, consist-
ing mostly of murderous rage toward the careless and irresponsible
teenager. She said she had an intense urge to grab her husband's
shotgun and "blow that girl's head off." After 2 hours of intense
abreaction, she was given a mild sedative, and she immediately fell
into a deep sleep from which she emerged 10 hours later to go into a
state of profound but normal grief.

Her inhibited murderous rage toward the killer of her child had
been converted into the physical symptom of intense headache, the

symbolic expression of her wish to "blow that girl's head off." Her conversion reaction was short-lived since the precipitating event was fresh, and the opportunity for immediate abreaction was fortunately available through the help of a trusted physician.

Another example of conversion reaction in a relatively normal person is the case of the medical student who ordinarily suffered from intense examination anxiety. He was in high spirits and good humor when he came to the breakfast table of his fraternity house on the morning of a final examination. Throughout the meal he was friendly, voluble, and expansive. His cheerful demeanor struck a discordant note in the dining room populated by expectably anxious and worried fellow students, and he was the target of numerous hostile remarks because of his state of exaggerated joviality and cheerfulness.

At the conclusion of the meal, as his fraternity brothers rose to face their examinations, he found himself unable to move. He could not arise from the table, and when assisted to his feet, his legs collapsed and he fell to the floor. His friends were alarmed, but the paralyzed student continued to display the high good humor that he had shown since he had entered the dining hall. He was rushed to the hospital emergency room by his anxious friends, where he became the focus of many diagnostic tests while his colleagues were being subjected to the stresses of a final examination.

This young man's anxiety about the examination had become intolerable, and his ordinary self-protective devices failed. The conflict was then converted into a physical paralysis. It served the dual purpose of avoiding the examination and expressing the state of abject helplessness which he routinely felt in the face of examinations. By ordinary standards, this young man was an adequate and effective person not given to neurotic illness. His paralysis was short-lived, it required no treatment other than reassurance, and to our knowledge it never recurred.

INHIBITION

General Comments

Although inhibition is not included in all lists of defense mechanisms, this mode of avoiding conflict is mentioned with sufficient frequency to warrant inclusion. The learning blocks of children and the work blocks of adults are common examples. The individual avoids conflict by giving up or failing to become involved in activities from which he would otherwise profit or derive pleasure. He avoids these activities either because they are symbolic representations of forbidden unconscious impulses or because they are activities in which such impulses are likely to be expressed. This resembles phobic behavior in which the patient constricts his sphere of activity to avoid objects or situations which he fears. Unlike phobias, however, inhibitions produce no clear sense of fear of the avoided activities; instead, the person using the defense mechanism of inhibition experiences only a lack of interest or lack of motivation to engage in those activities. Inhibition is somewhat similar to the loss of function characteristic of the motor paralysis of a conversion reaction. But instead of so obvious a symptom as paralysis, inhibition involves a more subtle avoidance of activities which is attributed to lack of interest in the activity or lack of skill to engage in it.

Definition

Inhibition refers to the involuntary and unconsciously instituted diminution or loss of motivation to engage in some activity in order to prevent anxiety over disowned and unacceptable impulses. The activity is often one which would otherwise be useful or enjoyable to the person, but he avoids it because it would stir up conflict over primitive forbidden urges by reminding him of the forbidden impulses or by tempting him to express them in behavior.

Clinical Examples

Example 1. A young married man, who idealized his wife, gradually lost interest in sexual relations with her, attributing his difficulty to worry over business problems and fatigue from overwork. While on business trips, he regularly engaged in sex with women he picked up at bars. This return of sexual interest on trips, he explained, occurred because he was then less burdened by the everyday problems in his office. In this case we see examples of the defenses of both inhibition and rationalization (see p. 56). In the course of psychotherapy it became clear that he unconsciously regarded sexual intercourse as a sinful and "dirty" act which a man should not engage in with a "nice" woman. As a consequence of this infantile attitude, he had lost interest in his wife, a "nice" woman, and could feel attracted only to the "bad" women whom he picked up in bars.

Example 2. A young man was an avid and skillful chess player, but with certain opponents he regularly tended to lose when play reached the point at which he could decisively defeat his opponent. This occurred when he played with men who tended to be easily angered if they lost at chess. In such games the patient would frequently be unable to see an obvious move by which he would take his opponent's queen or checkmate his king. An extended period of psychoanalytic psychotherapy revealed that these sudden episodes in which he was unable to see the right move were due to inhibition of his ordinary vigilance as a chess player. This defended against childish aggressive impulses to annihilate his opponent. These impulses were associated with equally primitive dread of retaliation— consciously experienced as a vague dread that his opponent would, if defeated, explode in rage, as the patient's father often did when bested in competition or when frustrated.

Example 3. An attractive young female patient lost interest in ballroom dancing and avoided parties where she might be called on to dance. Psychotherapy revealed that she had intense unconscious exhibitionistic wishes to behave in a sexually provocative way. To engage in the quasi-sexual activity of dancing tempted her to make a sexual spectacle of herself. To avoid that anxiety-rousing temptation, she lost interest in dancing. Consciously, she only knew that dancing was no longer enjoyable or of interest to her.

Example 4. A young man was referred for treatment because of his refusal to participate in physical education at his high school. The course required him to change into a gym suit in the locker room and to shower in a group shower stall. During his latency years he had developed a disabling dread of exposing his body and a morbid preoccupation with the idea that he was not as well developed physically as his peers. At puberty his dread of exposure was repressed. Although free of conscious conflict about it, he began to refuse to participate in any activity which required physical exposure, and his scholastic life assumed a warped character as a result. As long as he could avoid undressing in the presence of his peers, he behaved normally. When his avoidance techniques were challenged in high school, he elected to accept expulsion rather than to participate in physical education. The school authorities recognized the severity of the difficulty, and enlisted the aid of his family in seeking help for the young man.

Psychoanalytic treatment revealed that the patient had deep-seated and powerful conflicts about his strong competitive, exhibitionistic, and aggressive urges which he regarded as potentially overwhelming and dangerous. His intense fears of retaliation and punishment for indulging such urges caused him to block out the expression of any activities which even remotely related to those urges. Consequently, a major area of his existence was totally inhibited. He had no sense of fear of the locker room or shower stall; rather, he felt that compulsory physical education was "silly" and that he could better use his time in other educationally "worthwhile" things, like reading. Thus, rationalization (p. 56) was used in addition to inhibition.

Clinical Syndromes Which Illustrate Inhibition

The clinical syndromes or life circumstances in which inhibition may be observed are: (1) writing blocks and work blocks; (2) social shyness preventing participation in such activities as dancing, dating, athletics, and public speaking; and (3) reading and learning blocks.

Occurrence of Inhibition in Normal Behavior

The occurrence of this defense is common in normal people. All people are to some degree inhibited in certain activities or interests which they either tend to avoid or to participate in with some degree of irrational apprehension. Dancing, public speaking, or attempting to hit a golf ball in the presence of other people are examples.

Many people feel inhibited when asked to speak into a microphone, even when it is sending signals only into a dictating machine. Apprehension while speaking on public radio is understandable, but here too, anxiety is usually out of proportion with the circumstance and contains some irrational aspects. But clearly the fear of the microphone and the inhibition in using it when it is attached to a piece of dictating equipment is more irrational.

Relatively normal adults often have transient episodes during which they avoid reading the newspaper, going to movies, watching the news on television, or reading certain kinds of novels because of their need to avoid reminders of unpleasant or fearsome topics as crime, violence, sexuality, etc. These passing inhibitions usually occur during periods of stress, and such people wish in those moments to turn to light, diverting stories, movies, or television. They want to see and hear things far removed from inner impulses, feelings, and fears which may be threatening at the time. Such relatively normal behavior is essentially the same in its form and dynamics as that seen in a more extreme and persistent fashion in people who suffer a clearly pathologic degree of inhibition; for example, obsessional patients who are tormented by sexual or aggressive thoughts and avoid reading newspapers or watching movies or television programs, lest they contain references to sex or aggression. Any reminder of sex or violence makes them unbearably anxious because it threatens to make them aware of their own forbidden impulses, hence their lack of freedom to read or to watch drama. They suffer a massive inhibition of function to further defend against their own impulses. This may become so extreme that they give up reading altogether because ordinary and proper words have sexual or aggressive connotations, for example, *come, shaft, intercourse, pussy, prick, frigid, hot, make, destroy, knife, gun,* and countless others. Frequently, people who suffer either from a transient and relatively normal inhibition, or a more obviously pathologic and persistent one, are not aware of the reasons for their avoidance. They tell themselves and others that they avoid certain books, stories, movies, or activities because they do not find them interesting, or that they are too deep and not understandable. In such instances we see the use of the additional defense of rationalization (see p. 56) to explain the results of inhibition.

DISPLACEMENT

General Comments

The mechanism of displacement occurs in its clearest form in phobias, particularly in children. Anxiety over conflict related to an unconscious, previously repressed, forbidden impulse may call forth this additional defense mechanism when repression fails. As the impulse threatens to come into consciousness, it is displaced, that is, reconnected to some external situation which is a suitable symbolic representation of the impulse and yet sufficiently dissimilar so as to appear unrelated to it. This defense clothes a wolflike impulse in psychological sheep's clothing to prevent its true meaning from becoming consciously recognizable.

Like the conversion symptom, the phobia represents both the defense against a conflictual impulse and the symbolic expression of the impulse, but in a form sufficiently disguised to prevent conscious awareness of its true nature. Frequently, the objects and situations onto which impulses are displaced are, in fact, somewhat dangerous and are commonly feared, for example, storms, potentially dangerous animals, germs, high places, closed spaces, or lightning.

Definition

Displacement refers to the unwilled, unconscious process which attaches the threat stemming from an unconscious impulse to some external situation, person, object, or animal which is then felt to be the source of the threat. An inner threat which a person cannot avoid by repression is now perceived as an outer danger that is not obviously related to or caused by any unacceptable urges from within the person. He may now cope with the danger by avoiding the feared object or situation.

Clinical Examples

Example 1. The case of little Hans described in 1909 by Freud (1955a) is a classic example of childhood phobia. Hans was a 5-year-old boy who developed an extreme phobia of horses. He feared they would harm him in some way, in particular, by biting him. This occurred at the height of his Oedipal conflict when he felt great anger toward his father and wished for his death. While struggling with these feelings, the boy happened to see a horse fall in the street, kicking and making such noise that the child thought it was dying. The horse was wearing blinders which reminded the child of his father's heavy black-rimmed glasses, and the movement of the horse's mouth reminded him of his father's mustache as it moved when his father talked. The child's fear of his own Oedipal impulse to harm his father was repressed and displaced onto horses which he wished to see fall down and suffer. This, in turn, was replaced by his fear that in retaliation for his evil wish a horse would harm him.

Example 2. An intelligent, devout Catholic, and very dependent woman who had no other living family member to whom she could turn for help, felt trapped in an extremely unsatisfactory marriage to a dull, inconsiderate, and cruel man. Her husband left town for a pleasure trip at a time when his wife was about to deliver her sixth baby. While she was in labor, a hurricane struck. From this time on, the woman developed a progressively severe phobia of storms, even mild rainstorms. Her storm of rage toward her husband to whom she was bound by economic, religious, and dependency ties, was repressed, and the fear of retaliation in kind was displaced onto storms outside of herself. In this way, the woman avoided the intolerable conflict she would feel were she aware of her true feelings toward her husband with whom she felt forced to live for the rest of her days.

Example 3. A 30-year-old traveling salesman sought psychoanalytic treatment for a severe phobia which threatened his source of livelihood. He had become so fearful about driving his car over large bridges that he was forced to take long detours in order to seek out ferries or lower and smaller bridges to reach his destination. Because of his need to avoid large bridges, the number of miles he was required to travel in his territory had quadrupled within a year, and the amount of time he was forced to spend in transit greatly increased. He found himself planning his itinerary for weeks ahead to avoid certain bridges. He observed that the intensity of his phobia was directly proportional to the size of the bridge. In the course of his therapy, two interesting facts emerged: he had never had sexual contact with a woman, and in his masturbation fantasies he invariably pictured a woman who was clothed from the waist down. As these fantasies were analyzed, he became aware that the women in them were thus clothed because he had an intense, but not precisely defined, conviction that it was dangerous to look at things "below." With pressure from the therapist, the patient reluctantly attempted to explore his fear of looking at the female genitalia. He then developed a spurious preoccupation with homosexuality in an effort to demonstrate that he was, in fact, a homosexual and that investigation of his attitude about female genitalia was therefore unnecessary since he had no interest in them. It eventually became clear that his intense fear of the female genitalia was based on primitive and infantile curiosity about that part of his mother's body that was below. In a childlike manner he feared some awesome punishment for his urges to see what was below. This fear had been displaced to chasms and ravines which were below the bridges that he feared to cross. While crossing bridges he felt so compelled to look downward that he feared he might lose control of his car and plunge off the bridge into the river or ravine below.

Example 4.   The 18-year-old bride of a wealthy, self-centered, and immature young man sought help for a paralyzing fear of thunderstorms.

Immediately following her marriage, she had discovered that her new husband had a violent and uncontrollable temper which sent him into rages when he was crossed in the most trivial matters. Her inability to express anger at her husband was almost identical to her inability in childhood to express anger toward her father. When her phobia first occurred, she was at home alone during a thunderstorm, and she became so panic stricken that she was barely able to call her husband at his place of business to seek his support. His own bewilderment and anxiety at the plight of his new wife caused them to seek assistance, and she was referred for psychiatric help.

During the course of her therapy she recalled her early childhood terror at the sound of her father's voice. He was a physically huge and overpowering man who spoke in gruff, hearty tones. She had always found it difficult to distinguish his genial moods from his anger, since one seemed as noisy as the other. Because of her childlike fear of retaliation, she was never able to express dissatisfaction with or anger toward her father, and the unexpected temper outbursts on the part of her husband quickly touched on this sensitive but hitherto repressed area. When she found herself alone during a severe thunderstorm, primitive fears which she had originally experienced in her relationship with her father were displaced, resulting in fear of the storm with its bolts of lightning and rumbling thunder.

Clinical Syndromes Which Illustrate Displacement

Clinical syndromes or life circumstances in which displacement may be observed include phobias, particularly in children, and everyday instances of "kicking the cat" because of anger engendered elsewhere which could not be expressed.

Occurrence of Displacement in Normal Behavior

This mechanism is easily observed in the behavior of normal people. Probably because displacement is an innate characteristic of the primitive way in which children think, people easily tend to revert to it when faced with unpleasant adversity in their adult years. This tendency to revert to earlier modes of behavior and thought is taken up in greater detail in the section on regression (p. 73).

The use of displacement by normal people is exemplified by the man who is unable to express his anger at his boss, and who then later in the day berates his spouse or kicks the family cat. Another person, thing, or animal becomes the object of the impulse which for one reason or another he has been unable to express against its true target. The individual who uses displacement in this fashion does not attribute the danger associated with the impulse to the substitute object as occurs in the formation of a phobia. This kind of partial displacement involves only half the equation necessary for a phobia to develop and for displacement in its more obviously symptomatic form to occur. Furthermore, in the normal person the impulse is ordinarily conscious, and the person is usually able to see that he is deflecting an impulse on a substitute target. Displacement in this sense was exploited by a New York department store which for many years sold inexpensive plaster-of-Paris figurines called *Kigmes*. According to the advertisements, during moments of anger smashing a Kigme provided a safe outlet for feelings which might otherwise prove dangerous.

Another very common use of displacement by normal people, which closely approximates the obviously pathologic use of displacement in phobic neuroses, can be observed in individuals who have a mild fear of flying. Usually such people have little if any sense of apprehension about driving long distances in an automobile, especially if they do the driving. This is true even though one is in greater danger of death when traveling by automobile than by commercial aircraft. Obviously, such a mild phobia about flying is irrational from the point of view of statistical probabilities of danger. Its presence may be noticeable only in the banter that occurs among passengers in the cocktail lounge before they board the airplane. Apprehension from such a miniature phobia in one of the authors of this book produced an amusing slip of the tongue. As he joked with colleagues in the airport bar about his hope that the pilot of his flight was capable and in good health, a friend asked him what time his flight was. For a moment after answering, he was unaware that he had made a slip of the tongue. He had said, "My fright leaves at 3 PM." Although such miniature phobias do not significantly interfere with the usual business of life, they readily betray the presence of unconscious and infantile conflicts which have invaded and colored the adult's evaluation of a current situation. Once airborne, one is a helpless captive in the plane, and is indeed at the mercy of the pilot, the mechanics who worked on the plane, the men in the control tower, and the weather. The passenger depends on all these for his safety as totally as the small child does on the parent. Under such conditions, whatever unworthy and unconscious sexual or aggressive impulses that may be causing apprehension from inside, tend to be displaced and are experienced as potential threats from the outside.

RATIONALIZATION

General Comments

A mechanism of defense which is familiar to everyone is rationalization: the attempt to give a rational explanation for behavior which is, in fact, irrational and motivated by unconscious impulses or by defenses against such impulses. When consciously used to misrepresent the reasons for a particular action, rationalization does not deserve to be called a defense mechanism. It is then simply lying, or at best, excuse-giving. Rationalization may be considered a defense mechanism only when it is used without conscious intent. It is frequently used to justify behavior that results from the use of other defense mechanisms. An example of this use of rationalization was cited in the section on inhibition (the case of the high school student who refused to go to his gym class because he did not consider that it was educationally worthwhile, p. 49).

Many of the defense mechanisms, such as displacement and conversion can be viewed as second lines of defense used to bolster failing efforts to keep previously repressed, anxiety-producing impulses out of consciousness. Rationalization is often used as yet a third line of defense. A repressed impulse threatens to emerge into conscious awareness. Inhibition, displacement, or other defense mechanisms are called into play to keep the unacceptable impulse out of awareness. When the behavior that results from these defense mechanisms is unusual and comes to the attention of others, rationalization is often invoked as a third line of defense to provide a plausible explanation for the illogical behavior.

Definition

Rationalization refers to the unconsciously motivated and involuntary act of giving logical and believable explanations for irrational behavior motivated by unacceptable, unconscious wishes, or by the defenses used to cope with such wishes.

Clinical Examples

Example 1. A physician began to have difficulties in concentrating, and his clinical work with patients deteriorated as he became increasingly preoccupied with sexual matters. In taking histories from patients, he would dwell at great length on the minutiae of their sex lives, especially on matters related to perverse sexuality. When this preoccupation became a matter of concern to his colleagues, he explained that his behavior derived from his legitimate interest in the effect of human sexuality on physical and psychological health. At first his explanations were so sincere and plausible that his colleagues treated his behavior as unusual but not abnormal. When the doctor's behavior became so obviously irrational that his patients complained to other physicians, colleagues confronted him with the seriousness of the situation, and insisted that he seek psychiatric help. He became indignant, and quoted from various textbooks to support his view that his interest in the sexual life of his patients was a legitimate scientific and medical endeavor. He argued persuasively and logically, convincing some colleagues that he was perhaps right. When the medical society finally decided that he could no longer continue in practice, he became enraged at the colleagues who conveyed this decision to him. He argued persuasively that one of them was a disturbed man who for irrational reasons was treating him unfairly.

Here, we see the failure of repression of primitive and infantile sexual impulses—as all perverse sexual impulses are. They came to conscious awareness, and for a time were handled by projection and rationalization: it was his patients who were concerned about sex, and his interests were purely scientific. When initially confronted with his irrational behavior, he convincingly explained it away—a renewed use of rationalization. When finally told he must leave his practice, primitive rage came to the fore. The hate and destructive intent within him was then projected onto colleagues; it was they who had irrational wishes to damage his reputation. The irrational aspect of this projection was then defended against with yet another layer of rationalization so clever that some colleagues believed the doctor's paranoid ideas, and for a time thought that he was being accused unfairly.

Example 2.   Another example of rationalization is the previously cited case (p. 48) of the impotent man who gave his wife various logical sounding excuses when the defense of inhibition caused him to lose any sexual desire for her. The patient obviously believed his rationalizations and had no conscious intent of misleading his wife or misrepresenting the cause of his difficulty.

Example 3.   The wife of a successful and affluent professional man was referred for consultation because of increasingly severe and frequent squabbles with her husband. The possibility of divorce had entered the picture, revolving primarily around the issue of the wife's refusal to participate in social activities which the husband felt to be essential to his professional advancement.

During the early years of their marriage, the wife was able to socialize somewhat more freely than she was at the time of the referral, but she realized in retrospect that even then she was inclined to avoid social events whenever possible. She had worked out an elaborate explanation for this earlier behavior, insisting that she rarely had the proper clothes for socializing, and that strained financial circumstances during these early years did not permit her to acquire the proper wardrobe. Even after the husband had become financially successful, the wife clung to the explanation of improper and insufficient clothes to wear, and even more strikingly, she doggedly invoked the same explanation after she had personally been the recipient of a substantial legacy.

At the time of the psychiatric consultation she insisted that unreasonable pressure from her husband to participate socially was responsible for her initial refusal to comply, and that her ever-increasing recalcitrance was in response to ever-increasing unreasonable pressure from him. In short-term therapy the patient was able to see that for some years her meager and inadequate wardrobe could not be explained by inadequate finances, and that her husband's "pressure" had for the most part been in the form of patient and understanding encouragement and reassurance, with repeated offers to compromise, to make concessions, and to help in any way possible. With further exploration, the patient came to understand that her anxiety was less severe in the early years of her marriage because they participated in a lower socioeconomic stratum in which she felt more comfortable than at the present time. Eventually, she came face-to-face with her lifelong feelings of social inferiority and personal inadequacy which clearly stemmed from certain childhood conflicts. She had warded off the acknowledgment of these old conflicts through the use of a double rationalization: first, early in the marriage her inadequate wardrobe did not permit her to mix socially, and finances did not permit her a better wardrobe; second, even after she had sufficient money to buy the most fashionable clothing, her husband's "unreasonable" demands that she buy nice clothes was enough to make anyone refuse to do so. Thus, when her first rationalization lost its credibility, another took its place.

Example 4. A highly successful certified public accountant purchased from three to six new automobiles annually. He explained this behavior on the grounds that he often was able to get "special deals" because his accounting firm served several automobile agencies in the large city in which he lived; consequently, he argued that it was less expensive to trade for a new car than to have his old car repaired. His frequent purchases of automobiles became such a standing joke in the social circle in which he moved that whenever he made reference to some mechanical difficulty in the car which he then owned, sly and knowing smiles were passed around the group, to his considerable anger and embarrassment. He often found himself vigorously defending his recurring plan to trade for a new car on the grounds that the one he currently possessed was a "lemon." When he acquired the nickname "Lemon" at his country club, he realized that something was amiss in his behavior and sought psychiatric advice.

After many months of psychotherapy, this patient was able to come to grips with a profound sense of physical inadequacy which had plagued him since early boyhood. He was always of small stature, and as an adult he was only 5′ 5″, 120 lbs. In addition, he had suffered from a severe internal strabismus, only partially corrected by surgery, which had imposed limitations on many ordinary activities during his youth. When he became financially successful, he attempted unconsciously to compensate for his deep-seated feelings of physical inadequacy by driving only new and shiny cars which were totally free of any defect. When the slightest defect occurred in his new car, he was compelled to get a new one. He then rationalized his behavior on other grounds to avoid awareness of the true motivation for his neurotic need to buy cars.

Clinical Syndromes Which Illustrate Rationalization

Rationalization is almost invariably used to explain behaviors that result from the use of other defense mechanisms. It then serves as an additional defense to bolster a previously instituted but flagging mechanism of another sort. If such defensive behavior can be made to seem logical and realistic, the defensive function it serves is better disguised.

Occurrence of Rationalization in Normal Behavior

One of man's foremost conscious needs is to feel that his behavior is coherent and rational. Any behavior in ourselves that we view as irrational threatens our sense of sanity and mental integrity. When we behave in some inexplicable way, we are compelled to find a logical explanation for it, so that we can make sense out of what we think or do. When a person finds himself in this predicament he may resort to rationalization, and usually will.

REACTION FORMATION

General Comments

The defense mechanism of reaction formation is most clearly seen in obsessive and compulsive behavior. To ensure that some repressed disturbing impulse is kept out of conscious awareness or overt behavior, a person develops attitudes and behavior exactly opposite that which is being defended against.

Like mechanisms noted earlier (such as displacement and inhibition), reaction formation can be considered as a measure called into play to reinforce repression when it begins to weaken. The defense of reaction formation almost always involves a partial but symbolic expression of the repressed impulse: that is, it almost always has some of the characteristics of the very impulse whose expression it is designed to prevent. For instance, the trait of kindliness, when primarily organized as a reaction formation against impulses of cruelty, will have a rigid, inflexible, and inappropriate quality to it. It will be imposed on others under all circumstances, whether or not warranted. Consequently, it will have a bossy, coercive, and thinly disguised sadistic quality. The person who exhibits such reactive kindliness is a person who "kills with kindness."

Definition

Reaction formation refers to automatic and unconsciously motivated attitudes, behaviors, and feelings which are exactly opposite to unacceptable drives or feelings that the reaction formation defends against.

Clinical Examples

Example 1. After a period of obvious pleasure in being messy with food, or playing with mud or other "dirt," a little 3-year-old girl suddenly became extremely neat and fastidious. She wept if her hands, shoes, or clothing became soiled, and frantically insisted that her mother clean them. Such behavior is common in a child of this age.

Example 2. A 30-year-old woman, who as a child was stubborn and most difficult to toilet train, was clean and neat to a fault in her adult years. She maintained a spotless house, and was acutely uncomfortable in social situations at her home if an ashtray remained unemptied for more than a few minutes. Her extreme and inappropriate need for order and cleanliness burdened her friends and family who were unable to relax and enjoy themselves in her house because of her obvious distress if anything became even slightly soiled or disordered.

Example 3.   The sudden breakdown of reaction formation is apparent in the quiet, meek, "perfect" high school student who committed a sudden and impulsive murder. His reaction formation of extreme orderliness, kindliness, and propriety broke down under the pressure of the underlying hostility that had been defended against.

Example 4.   A 40-year-old attorney reluctantly sought psychiatric consultation on the advice of his internist. He had suffered for years from a peptic ulcer which had responded capriciously at best to medical management, and his internist suspected that emotional factors played an important role in the patient's medical problem.

This man divided his busy waking hours between his law practice and his activities on behalf of the League of Decency and other antivice leagues in a large metropolitan area. He was a powerful supporter of strict censorship of any form of erotica, but he devoted most of his energies to the eradication of "girlie" magazines and stag movies. He considered written pornography as offensive, but less dangerous to the public morals than "dirty" photographs and movies. His dedication to this project necessitated great vigilance over all newsstands and "skin flick" movie houses, and in the name of censorship he had accumulated a garage full of erotic magazines, and he had also become an authority on erotic films, all of which he condemned with monumental indignation.

Although his attempt at therapy was abortive, he presented enough of his early childhood background to shed light on his avid interest in censorship of the "obscene." When the patient was 6 years old, his brutal and drunken father apprehended him peering through the keyhole of a bedroom, watching his aunt undress. The father not only beat him severely, but shamed and humiliated him by exposing his nefarious deed to the other members of the family. In retrospect, the patient was thoroughly convinced of the wisdom and righteousness of his father's action, and attributed his own impeccable righteousness to this one particular event.

Another interesting fact which emerged during the few sessions of his unsuccessful treatment was that he and his wife had never engaged in sexual play, much less intercourse, during daylight hours. Although all of the details in this particular case are not at our disposal, it seems likely that this patient's intense childhood curiosity and interest in looking had been vigorously repressed. Repression was then further reinforced by a reaction formation through which the patient safeguarded himself and all of society from prurient curiosity. However, in the name of decency he was obligated to spend many hours perusing pornographic magazines and reviewing sexy movies. Thus, his reaction formation both gratified and defended against his infantile curiosity about sexual matters.

Clinical Syndromes Which Illustrate Reaction Formation

The clinical syndromes or life circumstances in which reaction formation may be observed include obsessive-compulsive neuroses, obsessive-compulsive character styles, and normal character formation in childhood.

Occurrence of Reaction Formation in Normal Behavior

Reaction formation occurs in the course of normal development in children. At approximately the age of 3, conscience begins to organize, and parental pressure to conform increases. The 18-month-old who screams and kicks in a rage, throws food about the room, masturbates, or sucks his thumb when lonely, is more usually consoled than punished. From about age 3 onward, such behavior is more likely to bring punishment than consolation. As the child develops controls over anger and childish sexuality, he struggles to master his own naughty, bad, or dirty impulses. For a time, he often overshoots the mark, and becomes unduly fastidious about cleanliness, and overly concerned about order and regularity. If he soils himself with food or feces, he is extremely distressed and demands to be cleaned and dressed in unsoiled clothes. If food is not arranged on the plate in the way he feels is proper, he will not eat. The urgency of his need for order and cleanliness, and for control over "bad" impulses betrays the defensive struggle he is making against childish wishes of a sexual or aggressive nature. Much of the useful and necessary self-discipline that fosters accomplishment in later life evolves from these reaction formations of childhood.

The rigorous discipline needed to write in a "clean," orderly, and lucid style or to draw an architectural plan skillfully and neatly is a cousin to pathologic reaction formation. One writes a page or draws a plan only to find the sentences are cluttered or the plan incorrect or smudged with ink. In exasperation he obscures the whole thing with scrawling marks of disapproval, or crumples the paper and throws it away. His efforts to bring order and clarity are repeated until he has organized his ideas in "clean" copy and in a satisfactory manner—similar to the insistence of the muddy 3-year-old to be cleaned and tidied.

All normal people have small areas of activity in which behavior akin to pathologic reaction formation occurs. Some otherwise normal women are unduly distressed if company arrives when the living room is not spic and span. Some men have a similar excessive need for their car or boat always to be immaculate. In these instances, living room, car, or boat are to some degree involved unconsciously in conflict over forbidden impulses that threaten to erupt. When the need to keep such items spotless is extreme and inflexible, the defensive function that it plays becomes readily apparent.

UNDOING

General Comments

Like reaction formation, undoing is characteristic of the obsessive-compulsive neuroses. Indeed, both of these defenses often occur in the same person and frequently merge into each other, as we will illustrate by additional data on the case of the fastidious housewife cited in the previous section on reaction formation. Her reaction of excessive cleanliness developed into a handwashing compulsion, an act of undoing.

Undoing is a two-step defensive act. In the first step, a forbidden impulse is either expressed in action (at least in some small way or in some symbolic form) or in thought (which may be unconscious or in a disguised, symbolic form). In the second step, another act is performed which symbolically cancels the impulse expressed in the first step. This second step occurs in the form of a compulsive ritualistic act which is designed to exert magical control over the feared impulse or its potential consequences. In some instances, the first step occurs completely outside of awareness and the second step, the act of undoing, is triggered by a completely unconscious threat that a feared impulse might erupt into awareness or action.

The magical nature of acts of undoing are similar to the rituals used by magicians. The compulsive neurotic attempts to ward off evil consequences of his feared impulses by the magic he imputes to his acts of undoing, much as a magician influences events by waving his wand and intoning, "Abracadabra!" Undoing is a secondary layer of defense which is evoked in response to a partial return of an already repressed impulse, or at times, the unconsciously perceived threat that such a return is about to occur.

Definition

Undoing refers to unconsciously motivated acts which magically and symbolically cancel, counteract, or otherwise reverse a previous act or thought which is motivated by an unacceptable unconscious impulse.

Clinical Examples

Example 1. The woman who was the immaculate housekeeper cited in the section on reaction formation developed a handwashing compulsion which illustrates the defense mechanism of undoing. When one of her children became severely ill with pneumonia, she became pathologically concerned about germs and dirt, and developed a handwashing compulsion which she explained as an action designed to protect the other members of her family against the spread of germs from her sick child. The handwashing became so extreme as to be incapacitating; it occupied so much of her time during the day that she had no time for her usual housework. These chores as well as the care of the sick child were then imposed on her husband and other children. Consequently, her compulsive sanitary precautions exposed the family to the very risk of infection against which the compulsive precautions were supposed to protect. The magical and infantile quality of her ritual is obvious; moreover, it simultaneously expressed both her hostile wishes to harm her family and the defense against such wishes.

Example 2. A 24-year-old man became increasingly obsessed with the idea that his angry thoughts might somehow cause harm. If in a moment of anger he thought, "I'd like to kill that guy," he would worry for days that the person toward whom the thought was directed might be killed in some accident. One rainy night while driving on an overpass which crossed a busy freeway, he saw a brick in the middle of the road. A few blocks later, the idea occurred to him that he might have hit the brick and knocked it off the overpass, causing it to crash into the windshield of a car on the heavily traveled freeway below, resulting in a bloody accident involving many cars. At considerable effort, he circled back to the overpass to see if the brick was still in the roadway. Arriving at the overpass 45 minutes later, he could not find the brick, and immediately thought that he surely had knocked it over and caused the bloody wreck of his fantasies. He stopped, looked below, but saw no wreck. Immediately he thought, "It might have happened and the wreckers have already removed the smashed cars." Thereupon, he felt compelled to phone every hospital in town to see if people injured in a car wreck at that particular location had been brought in. Only after several hours on the telephone could he feel easy enough to go to sleep.

In Example 2, we see the sequence of a thought of a destructive nature (I might have hit the brick and thus caused an accident) followed immediately by a compulsive and irresistible urge to go back to see if he had hit the brick or to remove it if it were still there. Thus, he attempted to undo a potential wreck by preventing it, or, if he had caused a wreck, he could undo its consequences by rendering aid and calling an ambulance. This is undoing of a kind similar to the handwashing compulsion of Example 1 in this section. In more complicated and obscure compulsions, there is a much less apparent relation between the forbidden impulse and the consequent act of undoing. Indeed, there may be no conscious awareness of any prior forbidden thought or impulse; only the compulsive act of undoing is consciously experienced.

Example 3. A late adolescent male complained of elaborate rituals which were so complex and time-consuming that they greatly interfered with the conduct of his life. For example, he required an hour or more to go to bed at night because he was compelled to arrange and then repeatedly rearrange his bed clothing, until pillows, sheets, blankets, and mattress were all in a certain complicated pattern. Each item of bed clothing could touch no more than the absolute minimum number of other items of bed clothing before he could get into bed.

During the course of therapy, he found that in his ordinary daily

routine he was also plagued by a morbid dread of touching. All his
activities were influenced by the same considerations he described
regarding his bedtime ritual. After many months, the touching prohibition was found to relate to his penis and to stringent prohibitions in
his childhood regarding the touching of his genitalia. Many such
touching prohibitions had continued since childhood, but there was
a sudden intensification of them at puberty. At that time, the patient
recalled that he took elaborate pains not to come into physical contact with his mother under any circumstances, and he was particularly careful never to pass her in a face-to-face position. The
elaborate rituals to rearrange all objects so that they touched mini-
mally were found to be ways of undoing his wish to touch his penis
to masturbate and to undo his wish to touch his mother sexually.

Example 4.   A 34-year-old patient, the mother of four children,
was passionately addicted to reading murder mysteries. She derived
her greatest pleasure from curling up for an afternoon with a detective novel and some tasty snacks, both of which she devoured,
brooking no interruptions. From time to time, she was overwhelmed
by an intense feeling of guilt for neglecting her children by devoting
so much time to reading. On these occasions, she found that she was
unable to finish the last chapter or two of the murder mystery which
she was eagerly reading. She would then feel very frustrated by the
thought that she must go forever without savoring the climactic
moment when the guilty person was revealed. This was her way of
doing penance for the neglect of her children. This is a less obvious
form of undoing than that in the previously cited case of the man
who was obsessed about striking a brick on the highway.

The mother addicted to detective stories unconsciously harbored powerful feelings of antagonism toward her children whom
she felt bound her in a miserable marriage to a man she had come to
hate. Although she was, in fact, an adequate mother, her implacable
conscience caused her to feel that she was neglectful and a bad
person who had to expiate her sins by periodically depriving herself
of some pleasure associated with her favorite indulgence—reading
detective novels. This form of undoing is similar to the behavior of
the repeater who periodically runs afoul of our system of criminal
justice. After the commission of his misdeed, the criminal is sent to
jail and is deprived of his liberty to do as he wishes, thus he pays his
debt to society. His crime is now forgiven—his previous hurtful acts

are canceled out, and, in that sense, undone. He then is free to repeat his crime until he is caught again.

Clinical Syndromes Which Illustrate Undoing

The clinical syndromes or life circumstances in which undoing may be observed include compulsive acts, such as handwashing, touching, counting, cleaning, and checking compulsions, and common, quasi-obsessional thoughts which normal people have at times, such as worry as to whether the stove was turned off before leaving home for a vacation. The potentially destructive negligence must be undone by returning to check.

Occurrence of Undoing in Normal Behavior

Most normal people occasionally resort to undoing. The widespread custom of knocking on wood immediately after expressing some optimistic wish is a good example. It betrays a more or less serious conviction that the gods will scowl on anyone who is so presumptuous as to be optimistic. The knocking on wood is a magical, symbolic act that appeases or defeats the gods. In a similar vein, some devout Catholics, when confronted with a threatening or distressing circumstance, instantly cross themselves in hope that God will help or forgive.

The custom of saying "Gesundheit" if someone sneezes is a similar magical act. Simple apologies after one has accidentally hurt someone else are of the same order. Saying, "I'm sorry" or "please excuse me" counteracts the preceding event. Indeed, if someone bumps into us and fails to undo his action symbolically with words of apology, we feel angry, even if the bump has been ever so slight.

The ritualistic use of a check list in an airplane prior to takeoff or landing is a realistic act akin to compulsive rituals. To be assured that some momentary lapse of memory or judgment does not cause the pilot to overlook some action necessary to the safety of the aircraft or to commit some act prejudicial to its safety, the pilot systematically (compulsively, if you like) has someone read each item on the check list, and he ritualistically says "check" as he assures himself he has attended to that item. In this way, some unconscious conflict, some unconscious impulse that might cause ᴉe pilot to forget or to behave in a dangerous way is better guarded ₃ainst. This realistic and rational "ritual" of the pilot stands in ϽΠtrast to the irrational compulsive ritual that a lady of our acᴉuaintance invariably performs before an airplane flight. She is comᴈlled to buy flight insurance in a particular fashion, as we will ᴈscribe in Chapter 6. If anything interferes with this ritual purᴂase, she becomes very apprehensive while flying.

ᴉOLATION OF AFFECT

General Comments

Isolation of affect is the mechanism of defense involved in the Ͻrmation of obsessional thoughts. It is a second line of defense ᴉlled into play when repression fails to prevent a disowned unconϽious urge from forcing its way into awareness. As repression fails, ᴉe aspect of the unconscious urge being defended against intrudes ᴉncontrollably into consciousness. But only the idea of the unconϽious and disowned sexual or aggressive urge is allowed into conϽiousness; the affect or feeling tone that would ordinarily ϽϽcompany such a thought remains repressed. Thus, the idea is ᴉolated from its appropriate affect. Shorn of affect, obsessional Ꞁeas do not seem quite real; they do not feel as if they belong to the ᴈrson having them since he experiences no corresponding emotion. 'or example, a young mother who has the obsessional thought, 'Kill the baby," finds her murderous thought repugnant and forᴉgn. She has no conscious wish to hurt her infant; she experiences ᴉone of the rage or hate appropriate to such a murderous thought. 'he idea seems strange, but she is incapable of preventing its ocᴉurrence. Although the obsessional thought of killing her baby is Ͻrmenting, frightening, and engenders guilt, the distress it produces ᴉ much less than the overwhelming anxiety that such a murderous ᴉought would produce if it were accompanied by intense feelings of ᴉge and hatred toward the infant. The defensive value of isolation ᴈs in the successful repression of affect.

Most obsessional thoughts have obvious sexual or aggressive ᴉnplication even though they are not accompanied by erotic or anᴦy feelings. The case of the "Rat Man" described in 1909 by Freud ᴈ955b) is an excellent example. The patient was obsessed with the thought that unless he paid a small debt owed to a friend, an ur speakable fate would befall his fiancee—she would be tied seated 1 a pot full of rats which would gnaw into her anus. When patien have obsessional thoughts which are not obviously sexual or aggre sive in nature, the thoughts regularly prove to be well-disguise versions of thoughts which do have such implications.

Definition

Isolation of affect refers to the unconsciously instituted, aut matic, and involuntary separation of the idea of an unconscious in pulse from its appropriate affect, thus allowing only the idea and n the associated affect to enter awareness. By allowing into consciou ness only the idea (devoid of its appropriate affect) a person ca avoid acknowledging the reality of or the responsibility for his in pulses. The impulses are then experienced only as alien ideas; the do not really belong to the person; he does not really feel them.

Clinical Examples

Example 1. A patient who harbored intense, unconsciou childish sexual curiosity was repeatedly shocked to find herse wondering, while in church, what the minister looked like witho clothes. The content of an obviously sexual impulse toward th minister came into awareness, but no feeling of sexual curiosity of pleasurable sexual anticipation accompanied the thought; i stead, the predominant affect was a feeling of shock or revulsion having such an outlandish idea.

Example 2. A young woman developed the tormenting bla phemous obsessional thoughts, "Shit on God," "Fuck God," "Go fucks Jesus," and "Jesus Christ, Supershit." She was appalled 1 find herself thinking such things, and feared that having suc thoughts was an unpardonable sin. Her parents were frequentl absent during her childhood, and she had been reared in an excee ingly moralistic manner by a maid who was primarily responsible fc her care. Whenever the patient misbehaved, the maid called her a kinds of vile names throughout childhood and adolescence. An alcc holic uncle who also lived in the house forced her into an overtl incestuous relationship which endured from the time she was years of age until she was 14. She recalled no feeling about these events, and recounted them as if they had happened to someone else. The rage and contempt which she felt toward her uncle, as well as the incestuous nature of her relation to him, was obvious in the symbolic meaning of her blasphemous thoughts. They furthermore referred to homosexual tendencies ("God fucks Jesus"), something she feared in herself because her traumatic childhood sexual experiences caused her to feel revulsion in adulthood whenever a man made any sexual overture to her. She erroneously interpreted her revulsion at heterosexuality to mean she might be homosexual.

Example 3. During the course of an analytic hour a 32-year-old male patient chuckled briefly, and stated, "I just had the thought of splitting your skull with an ax, but of course I don't mean it." The feeling of slight amusement which accompanied this fantasy highlighted the fact that the real and appropriate emotion was somehow not available to the patient at the moment in which the thought occurred. However, the thought was not sufficiently alien to enable the patient to disown it entirely. He therefore felt it necessary to indicate that although it was his own thought, he "did not really mean it."

This is a clear-cut instance of a primitive hostile impulse emerging in consciousness, but in a form essentially detoxified in that the emotion appropriate to such a murderous idea was cut off or "isolated" from the verbal content of the fantasy. In this way, the patient had protected himself against the full impact of his "Lizzie Borden" wish to split the analyst's skull.

Example 4. The 39-year-old father of three children, one of which was an 8-year-old daughter, reported with much anguish and embarrassment that the senseless thought of his daughter sucking his penis had entered his mind the previous evening. He recounted that he had come home after work to a cold and empty house, and while he was changing into lounging clothes, his 8-year-old daughter had brought him the evening newspaper and had asked if he needed anything else. After appropriate expressions of thanks for her thoughtful act, the fantasy of fellatio suddenly flashed into his mind, but in reporting it to the analyst he stated, "It was not an erotic fantasy; there was no feeling at all." It seemed quite clear that the feeling tone or human emotion that accompanied or preceded this fantasy had been split off from the patient's awareness, so that the content could occur "in isolation," that is, shorn of its affective component.

Clinical Syndromes Which Illustrate Isolation of Affect

The clinical syndromes or life circumstances in which isolation of affect might be observed include patients who suffer from obses sional ideas, the initial stage of normal grief during which the be- reaved realizes that someone close to him has died, but feels numl and devoid of feeling about the death, and the commonplace obser vation that "time heals all wounds." Traumatic events, such as frightening war experiences, cannot be talked about shortly after their occurrence without reliving intense and disturbing emotions In time, however, the person is able to speak dispassionately of these events without the recurrence of vivid and distressing affects.

Occurrence of Isolation of Affect in Normal Behavior

The capacity to isolate affect from thought is not only normal but necessary for the highest form of mental functioning—logic. To be able to use "cold" and precise logic, one must not be swayed by "hot" passions. In the mental combat between attorneys in the courtroom, each adversary attempts to demolish the other with compelling logic and cool, legal expertise. Indeed, if tempers fly or passions become too heated, the judge admonishes the adversaries, or interrupts the proceedings until the attorneys cool off.

Actors and lecturers who speak with so little feeling as to be monotonous and boring are engaging in behavior which, although not clearly abnormal, comes close to the pathologic defense of isola- tion of affect. Such a person may say all of the right words to convey a compelling point, but his inability to speak with "feeling" robs him of power to influence his audience.

The precursor of pathologic isolation of affect in adults occurs in the normal development of language and thought in children. Vocalization, which precedes verbalization, is predominantly a way of expressing feelings. The use of words begins around various emotionally charged need states such as hunger or the tension the child feels when he is in pain or has to urinate or to defecate. His first words, such as "Ma-ma," "Da-da," and various childhood words for food, urination, or defecation, are endowed with magical properties. He speaks the word to express a need and the parents come to his assistance. In the period between 3 and 6 years of age, the child endows words and gestures with magical powers, usually potentially harmful powers. The childhood rhyme, "Sticks and stones may break my bones, but words will never hurt me," reflects the child's struggle to refute his belief in the power of words. He attempts to disavow the ominous magical power of gestures by means of the childhood game, "Step on a crack and break your mother's back." In these ways he seeks to reassure himself that neither his thoughts nor his magical gestures have real power, and to establish firmly the more realistic belief that only sticks and stones can hurt—words cannot. But words and ideas can have great impact, and they can hurt or please—according to the feeling with which they are said. The words, "I love you," can be said with such tenderness as to leave no doubt in the mind of the beloved; or with such lack of feeling as to mean "I hate you." Or the words, "I hate you" can be said with an intonation and affect that makes them clearly mean, "I am very fond of you." But this kind of power which words have is not the magical power which the child fears and sometimes believes he possesses. Unconsciously, all adults harbor some vestiges of the childhood belief that words are magically endowed with power to harm or help. Regression to this belief in the magic of words is present in the obsessional neurosis.

REGRESSION

General Comments

Like displacement and projection, regression may be considered a general principle or attribute of mental functioning which at times may also serve to defend against conflict. It is discussed here in its capacity as a defense mechanism. The tendency to avoid unpleasantness in the present by a return in thought and in feeling to the past can be seen in the nostalgia people feel toward the "good old days." Elderly people tend more and more to live in the past as the ends of their lives approach and as their mental faculties wane.

When faced with some current unpleasantness, children are particularly prone to revert to modes of thought, feeling, and behavior characteristic of their earlier years. By functioning as they did when they were younger, they take the psychological position that the present adversity is not yet upon them.

Hypnosis provides one of the clearest examples of the capacity of normal people to regress under certain circumstances. A good hypnotic subject can be induced to regress to earlier levels of functioning by the suggestion that he is becoming younger and younger, and that he is beginning to experience and react to things in the same manner he did as a child. When regressed to a young age, say 4 years old, the total pattern of behavioral responses of the subject, including his performance on psychological tests, makes it quite clear that he has, very literally, returned to the modes of thought and feeling characteristic of early childhood. His response to psychological tests shows beyond doubt that he is not pretending to be younger, since the results, especially on projective tests such as the Rorschach, could not be simulated. His test record is practically identical to that of a child of the age level to which he has been regressed.

Definition

Regression refers to the automatic and unwilled reversion to modes of psychological functioning which are characteristic of earlier life stages, especially childhood years. This tendency to go back to earlier modes of functioning occurs when an individual is faced with some serious conflict in the present. The symbolic return to former years enables a person to avoid the present adversity and treat it as if it has not yet arrived.

Cinical Examples

Example 1. A previously well-adjusted 6-year-old boy reacted violently to the birth of a sister. At first, the boy exhibited intense anger and jealousy toward the newcomer. This show of antagonism was harshly criticized by his parents, and quickly disappeared, whereupon, the child became helpless, demanding, and less self-sufficient. Although he had formerly dressed himself, fed himself, and taken care of his toilet needs, he now began to soil himself, and became generally helpless. He obviously envied his baby sister. He demanded that his mother clean up his body and his messes as she did for the sister, and that she dress and feed him. He was again a little baby instead of a big boy. In this manner, he tried to regain the position of an infant on whom parents lavish attention, thus lessening his envy and intense rage toward the new baby.

Example 2. The behavior of the previously described obsessive-compulsive patient (p. 65) who feared that his hostile thoughts might cause physical harm to other people is an example of regression. He reverted to a level of functioning in which he could not clearly distinguish between the reality of a thought and that of an actual deed—a confusion characteristic of small children.

Example 3. Stuart Miller (1962) has cited a case in which regression occurred in a dramatic form under even more dramatic circumstances. The case was that of a prisoner of the Nazis who was tortured and endlessly interrogated while being made to stand for hours in a cellar filled with the stench of excrement. Suddenly, to his amazement, he found himself on a beautiful island. The air was fragrant with the scent of flowers. At first he was elated, and then, as he again realized where he really was, he became terrified that he was losing his mind. Initially, his regression to the level of magical thought characteristic of early childhood was involuntary. Later he became able to reproduce the experience at will and to use the regressive fantasy as a welcome escape from his grim reality. As we will note later, such deliberate and controlled regression is termed *regression in the service of the Ego.*

Example 4. A 50-year-old woman became acutely psychotic under the stress of a number of extremely traumatic events. As her physician talked to her, she refused to answer certain questions, stating that the yellow color of the chair in which she was sitting was commanding her to be silent on those topics. When asked how a color could control her so completely, she described at length the way that this particular color felt about her, and how the color had desires and wishes at times which were so strong that she had to do what the color wanted her to do. She had regressed to the animistic stage of thought characteristic of small children who attribute human characteristics to inanimate objects.

Example 5. A 42-year-old housewife began treatment because of severe anxiety and spells of depression. When anxious or depressed, she drank excessively. Her personal life was chronically chaotic because of the behavior of her very withdrawn and hostile husband, her rebellious and willful daughter, and her fumbling, ineffectual son. When even small increments of additional stress occurred, she would regress to exceedingly childlike and infantile modes of behavior. On several occasions, when confronted with a crisis in her life, she immediately began to talk babytalk, to use a limited and childlike vocabulary, and to think in a very concrete fashion. She sat crosslegged on the floor in the kitchen to eat her meals, which she did mostly with her hands. If she attempted to use a spoon or fork, she held it awkwardly as a toddler does. She smeared her body and the floor with food. The pitch of her voice and the expression on her face became remarkably similar to that of a 2- or 3-year-old. These acute episodes of regression usually lasted no more than a few days, clearing completely when she was hospitalized. Once the acute regressive episode was over, the patient was completely amnesic regarding it, but usually she could remember having been particularly disturbed by some life crisis prior to the episode. Although this case serves as an example of regression, it is also an example of dissociation, a defense mechanism described in a later section (p. 90).

Clinical Syndromes Which Illustrate Regression

Clinical syndromes or life circumstances in which regression may be observed most clearly are twofold. First, any patient who has a clinically manifest neurosis or psychosis will show evidence of regression in some area of his psychological functioning. A patient with a single circumscribed obsession, compulsion, or phobia may function in most other areas of his life at a very high level of maturity, manifesting obvious regression only in matters directly related to his symptoms. Psychoses involve a more pervasive regression which may affect almost all of the person's psychological functions. But usually even the most disturbed psychotic will retain areas of intact ego functioning. For example, a scientist who suffered a manic psychosis wrote a very lucid and coherent scientific paper while committed to a locked psychiatric ward. Although grossly out of contact with reality concerning matters related to his failure to attain academic promotion, the event which precipitated his psychosis, he was quite intact and competent in other areas of his professional activity.

Second, severe and extended physical illness always produces some degree of regression. By the very act of becoming hospitalized, a patient relinquishes a number of his adult responsibilities and activities. This alone fosters some regression. If he is seriously ill, a patient is cared for by others much as if he were a child. He then reverts in some measure to a childlike self-centered attitude, becomes less interested in things or people unless they are relevant to his care, tends to be impatient and irritable if frustrated, and becomes more needful of attention from others. If his illness necessitates absolute bedrest, especially if he must be assisted like a baby to bathe and perform toilet functions, the tendency to regress will be increased. He will expect his physician to be omnipotent, much as a small child expects his parents to be. The longing for magical help and protection under such circumstances is further discussed in Chapter 5 on the use of defense mechanisms in normal behavior. Such temporary childlike turning oneself over to the care of others is often necessary if one is to receive proper medical care. As every experienced doctor knows, no patient is more difficult to treat than a sick physician. The physician-patient often is less able or less willing to place himself in the role of a patient who, to a reasonable degree, lets his physician take charge of his life and direct his activities.

Occurrence of Regression in Normal Behavior

Periodic regression is not only observable in the behavior of normal people but also it is essential for the maintenance of psychological health. Everyone regresses each night in sleep. Thought, as manifested in dreams, takes on all of the primitive characteristics of the thoughts of small children. Concreteness, animism, omnipotence, and egocentricity are its hallmarks. To be able to retreat from reality as we sleep each night seems to be essential if we are to effectively face the demands of the day.

Similarly, most adults need to retreat periodically into daydreams in which the events that occur in their imagination are completely under their control and can be managed as they wish. If someone has experienced a slight or a humiliation at the hands of another person under circumstances in which he cannot fight or talk back, daydreams of triumph over his foe greatly assist in digesting the impact of the trauma. He can, in his imagination, continue for hours or days to re-enact the event, and each time he can carry it to a triumphant conclusion which he did not achieve in the actual event. He will humiliate his adversary with a sharp comment, or make a fool of him with brilliant logic.

The ability of the mature adult to enjoy leisure time and to indulge periodically in playful childlike activities is essential to mental health. On vacations or weekends the adult may retreat from reality, and play in a regressive fashion. But this healthy regression is under his control, and has been aptly designated by Kris (1952) as "regression in the service of the Ego." It is something he allows himself to do, and is in sharp contrast to the unwilled and involuntary nature of regression when it is used as a defense mechanism.

DENIAL

General Comments

The primitive defense mechanism, denial, occurs frequently in normal young children. When an adult resorts to denial as a preferred and persistent mode of dealing with painful reality, it is an ominous indicator of a severe disturbance in his capacity to assess reality correctly, and may well be evidence of a psychosis.

Definition

Denial refers to the automatic and involuntary exclusion from awareness of some disturbing aspect of reality or the inability to acknowledge its true significance.

Clinical Examples

Example 1. A baby died in a fire while his mother barely escaped from the house after making an unsuccessful attempt to rescue the child. She was badly burned herself, and when she finally escaped from the burning house, she realized that her attempt to rescue her child had failed. By the time she arrived at the hospital for the treatment of her burns, she insisted that the child had been saved by a neighbor and taken to another hospital, despite her former awareness that the child had not been rescued.

Example 2. The scientist who developed an agitated, manic reaction when he failed to get a faculty promotion (as noted in the section on regression, p. 76) made plans to establish a new, interdisciplinary study center where leading scientists would work together. He, of course, would be the president of the center, would invest considerable amounts of money in the venture, and would persuade numerous friends to invest also. He completely ignored the many financial, organizational, and academic barriers that stood in the way of such a scheme. He minimized and explained away such obstacles and problems so as to deny their existence as well as to deny his intense disappointment at his failure to achieve the rank of professor. Despite his severe psychosis, while hospitalized he wrote a lucid paper that was later published in a scientific journal.

Example 3. An elderly widow was hospitalized for an acute condition requiring a minor surgical procedure. During her brief stay in the hospital, she was intensely fretful and agitated about the welfare of her husband whom she felt would be helpless without her. Her surgeon, aware that her husband had died several months previously, asked for a psychiatric consultation.

The patient spoke at length of her retired husband's fumbling efforts to care for himself, and expressed the fear that he would be unable to attend adequately to his own needs during her absence. When the psychiatrist commented that he understood her husband had died several months earlier, the patient responded with a blank but indulgent stare and continued to talk as if her husband were alive. During a subsequent house call, after the patient had returned home, the psychiatrist discovered that the patient maintained a household routine oriented around the presence of two persons, including a place setting for two at the dining room table. Although this elderly lady proved perfectly capable of looking after herself and conducting her business affairs, she had instituted a circumscribed area of denial surrounding her former husband's death, which she was totally unable to acknowledge.

Example 4. Anyone who has had some exposure to children is familiar with the disavowal, "It wasn't me!". Even when caught with his hand in the cookie jar, the small child will vehemently invoke this disclaimer.

Clinical Syndromes Which Illustrate Denial

Clinical syndromes or life circumstances in which denial may be observed include:

1. Patients with fatal illnesses who deny their impending death
2. Severely burned patients who deny the severity of their burns and the future deformity which will result
3. Parents of a psychotic child or a dying child who refuse to acknowledge the severity of the child's disorder
4. The refusal by the spouse of a psychotic or addicted person to acknowledge the disturbance in the spouse
5. Ordinary grief which prompts one to say, "I can't believe that he is really gone," reflecting the inability to acknowledge that the death has occurred

Occurrence of Denial in Normal Behavior

Under certain conditions, normal people do not perceive aspects of their environment which are obvious to others. People do this when they do not want to be aware of some aspect of reality. For such people to be considered relatively normal, their use of denial must be reasonably transient, or involve some minor matter, and it must be capable of correction by information that clearly refutes the denial.

Intense concentration of attention on a task necessitates the exclusion of other aspects of reality not relevant to the task at hand. A student studying hard for an examination may not hear the radio playing next door or the telephone ring, or realize that the clock says that it is time for a date. In a measure, he denies the presence of reality, and must do so to some degree to study effectively. But his exclusion of certain aspects of reality from awareness is under his control. If someone says, "The phone is ringing, answer it!" he can become aware of reality. His denial of reality is not beyond his control, as it is in people suffering from overtly pathological mental states.

A somewhat less reversible and controllable denial is exemplified by a student who argued for weeks that gossip about his favorite professor was not true. The professor was having an obvious sexual affair with a female classmate of the young man. Although the facts were apparent, the student who denied them did not want to see the truth because he idealized the professor. After some weeks, he accepted the truth of the gossip, and was painfully disillusioned by his hero's behavior because it violated the student's idealized image of the professor, whose behavior evoked memories of the way that the student's father behaved when the student was a small child. This had left him with a deep unconscious hatred toward his father. The professor's behavior threatened to revive the unconscious rage from the student's childhood. But the conflict over unconscious rage was not so intense as to prevent the student from finally perceiving the truth.

Denial, even of a very massive type, may be normal when it occurs at very early periods of personality development. The child between the ages of 3 and 6 is notoriously prone to deny reality as his vivid imagination sweeps him into fantasies, or as reality threatens in some painful way. The 4-year-old who breaks the cookie jar may deny that he did the damage. With all honesty he may insist that someone else was the culprit, even an imaginary playmate.

The use of denial between the ages of 15 and 25, especially in young men, may be essential to normal development of personality at that period. To achieve mastery of themselves and their relation to the world, young people must experiment in various ways. They are compelled to see how fast an automobile will go, or how far into the ocean they can paddle their surfboards. To do this without undue apprehension they must deny the possibility that anything bad could possibly happen to them.

The adaptive necessity for denial in young men is seen most clearly in war time. No one can easily face the idea that he might be killed and still willingly place himself in a situation in which he is endangered. For example, denial allows young men to pilot airplanes with great skill in extremely dangerous circumstances. If they fully realized the danger they face, it might interfere with their capacity to be skillful pilots, thus impairing their chances of survival. They might become jumpy and erratic, and therefore run an even greater risk of death. Some pilots who were excellent flyers in World War II were so cautious in combat when recalled to service in the Korean conflict that they were not effective fighters. Ten years older, they more clearly grasped the danger they faced, and were appropriately apprehensive about it. When younger, their effectiveness as combat pilots had been enhanced because they denied the danger of combat.

PROJECTION

General Comments

Like denial, projection is one of the more primitive defense mechanisms. When it occurs in the extreme form of psychotic delusions and hallucinations, it is both dramatic and obvious. If used persistently regarding matters of significance in a person's life, projection is an ominous sign of psychotic disturbance. More frequently, it is the subtle and often socially disruptive mechanism exhibited in the widespread tendency of the relatively normal person to attribute to others those feelings, wishes, and attitudes in himself which he wishes to disown. Children, in particular, tend to claim ownership of their own laudable qualities and to attribute all of their faults and shortcomings to others, often making use of imaginary playmates for this purpose. Imaginary playmates very frequently are the representations of the "bad" aspects of the child's own feelings and urges. Selma Fraiberg (1959) describes the delightful instance of the "Laughing Tiger," an imaginary companion of her niece, age 2 years and 8 months. On one occasion the child firmly commanded "Laughing Tiger" to remain at home as she left with her uncle to visit the ice cream store. "Laughing Tiger" was not allowed to go to this place of pleasurable self-indulgence with his young mistress because, she stated, " . . . he has to learn to mind. He can't have everything his own way." This lesson in discipline was, of course, exactly what the tiger's young mistress was herself struggling with at that point. Her conflict over her own greed (after all, tigers eat voraciously and indiscriminately) and hostility (they also hurt people) was lessened by attributing these urges to "Laughing Tiger" (whoever saw a laughing tiger who was really bad?) whom she controlled completely with her commands.

Furthermore, when children at this age have an imaginary playmate such as "Laughing Tiger," they have a ready-made explanation for all the unfortunate things that happen for which the child himself is responsible. All naughty and punishable deeds can be blamed upon the antics of a "Laughing Tiger." A 3-year-old boy of our acquaintance had an imaginary playmate named "Pooh-Pooh Pot." Pooh-Pooh Pot was responsible for all mud tracks on the carpet, spilled milk, broken glassware or other household mishaps that frequently occurred in remarkable proximity to the young man.

The child often attributes to the parents as well as to imaginary playmates various unpleasant or fearful attitudes, ascribing to them, for example, his own rage and hate. Because of this process, they seem to the child to be more stern, threatening, and hostile than they really are. He then identifies with this fantasied sternness. Thus, after projecting his own hostile urges onto his parents, he then internalizes a punitive and threatening image of them which gives him, at least for a time, a harsher and more vindictive voice of conscience than his parents usually intend for him to have. He may also endow his parents with his own omnipotence, an attribute so obvious in the fantasy and play of the 4-year-old who, by an act of the imagination, effortlessly transforms himself into a mighty soldier or a healing nurse.

This tendency to project one's own attitudes onto others is always involved in any meaningful relation with another person. We consider this process a defense mechanism rather than a general characteristic of mental functioning only when it is used to avoid conscious awareness of forbidden unconscious impulses by attributing them to others. Projection can be considered as a second line of defense, evoked when repression fails. Like other such defenses, projection also involves a return of the repressed impulse, but now attributed to others. When projection has occurred, the person often resorts to rationalization to give the appearance of plausibility to the irrational projection.

Definition

Projection refers to the automatic and unconscious attribution of one's disowned attitudes and urges to some external agent, usually a person or persons.

Clinical Examples

Example 1. A young man was tormented by the delusional

belief that others were saying he looked like a homosexual. In this way he attributed his own doubts about his masculinity to others.

Example 2. One of the authors of this book was a passenger in an automobile driven by a colleague enroute to the driver's office. Since they were late, the driver was hastening as he pulled into his familiar parking space. Because of his haste, the driver miscalculated as he came to a stop, and his front wheels struck the curb rather violently, whereupon the driver exclaimed, "Damn that curb!" The passive, immobile, and inoffensive curb had certainly not changed position, much less attacked the wheels of the automobile, but the driver attempted to remove blame from himself by attributing it to the nonparticipating curb.

Example 3. The 36-year-old mother of three children explained her unpopularity in her neighborhood on the grounds that other mothers who were neglectful of their own children, envied and hated her for being such a good mother. Consequently, she said, they maliciously or wrongfully accused her of the very neglect of which they were guilty. She bitterly complained that they had somehow succeeded in convincing her husband of the truth of their vicious and unfair lies.

The facts were that the patient had been coerced into seeking psychiatric consultation by her husband, who had actually threatened to report her to the welfare department because of her blatant neglect of their children during his absences, which were frequent but unavoidable because of the nature of his work. She categorically denied his allegations, and defended herself by attributing to others the neglect and incompetence of which she was guilty.

Example 4. A 49-year-old man had struggled since early adolescence with intense conflict over homosexual urges. An early marriage had endured for 20 years, despite his sporadic, but increasing homosexual encounters. From the age of 40, at which time he was divorced, the patient had been exclusively homosexual, and strove to convince himself that this was the "highest" form of sexual expression. This hard won belief was precarious, and the patient had to reinforce it continually. As a consequence, he developed the conviction that all persons of prominence (political, scientific, social, or otherwise) were homosexual. This belief served as a justification for his own homosexual activities which basically he still wished to disown.

Clinical Syndromes Which Illustrate Projection

Paranoid delusions and hallucinations are prime examples of the use of projection. The hostile or sexually provocative behavior that the delusional patient attributes to other people are disavowed aspects of his own impulses. The auditory or visual hallucinations that he experiences represent projected thoughts and feelings he has about himself. Frequently, such a projection is so disguised that its relation to his own impulses and urges is obscure. Careful investigation, however, will invariably demonstrate that such phenomena are indeed projections of the person's own repudiated impulses and motivations.

Occurrence of Projection in Normal Behavior

The occurrence of projection in normal people stems from the universal tendency of the small child to attribute all that is bad to others and to claim as his own all that is good and proper. The imaginary playmate of the 3-year-old is not only a friend who prevents loneliness but also the culprit who is responsible for spilling milk at the table, breaking his father's tools in the garage, and doing hurtful things to pets and smaller siblings when the parents are not looking. The inability of the young child to distinguish clearly between the reality of a thought and the reality of a deed permits easy disavowal of personal responsibility for bad impulses. His egocentrism helps in the process in that it causes him to assume that everyone else thinks and feels as he does, consequently his projections will seem as plausible to them as they are to him.

The adult tends to perpetuate the illusion that all that is good and valuable is his own, whereas all that is bad and forbidden is attributed to someone else. Very few motorists who are caught speeding will agree that the patrolman who gave them a ticket was justified, and that they themselves were doing something foolish and illegal.

In adolescence, one sees the use of projection in a form so

intense that it obviously would be pathological if it were to occur in a mature adult. The adolescent, so egocentrically absorbed in his own feelings and his own struggle to disentangle himself from childhood and to face the responsibilities of adulthood, is unable to genuinely and consistently be concerned about the feelings and needs of others. Consequently, he frequently voices the complaint that, "No one around here really understands me or cares about what I feel or think." In this fashion, his own egotistical self-absorption is disowned and attributed to others. The cruelty of adolescents to each other is similar in its origin. The young adolescent boy, uncertain of his own masculinity, delights in tormenting others who are sissies. The adolescent girl, so uncertain of her own attractiveness as a woman, belittles the imperfections of her friends.

Dealing with projection is an important facet of psychotherapy. Although the psychotherapist seeks to maintain a nonjudgmental attitude of friendly neutrality, the patient often comes to feel irrationally convinced that the therapist will be critical of him. The psychotherapist must then help the patient see that he has projected onto the therapist some aspect of his own irrationally punitive and vindictive conscience. When the patient comes to feel that the neutral and relatively noncommittal therapist has sexual designs on him, the therapist has the opportunity to help the patient see that it is his own sexual feelings toward the therapist that are causing him concern. In this way, the patient may slowly realize how his projective tendencies distort his relations with people other than the therapist. When this aspect of the treatment succeeds, the patient gradually comes to grips with his own unwanted impulses rather than defending himself by attributing those impulses to others.

TURNING AGAINST THE SELF

General Comments

Turning against the self is a defense used against aggression. It stems from behavior that characterizes the earliest months of life and which only later comes to be used as a mechanism of defense. Helpless when needs are frustrated by the absence of the need-satisfying person, the small child may take action on his own body in an effort to alleviate his tension. When an unsatisfied need produces sufficient tension, an infant responds with a diffuse ragelike action—thrashing about, crying, kicking, and intense sucking, biting, or scratching on his own body. This early response provides the pattern for later turning against the self as a way of alleviating tension from an unconscious hostile impulse, thus sparing the person conscious awareness of either his own rage or the object of it, or both. Later versions of turning against the self are severe fingernail biting, scratching, head banging, accident proneness, intentional self-mutilation, and finally, suicide.

In this last instance, the most extreme form of turning against the self, the rage toward the other person is frequently betrayed in the bitter notes left for the hated survivor. These notes contain statements such as "I hope you realize now how much you have hurt me over the years of our miserable marriage. Now you can never hurt me again, you bastard." As the studies of Karl Menninger (1938) suggest, in this form of suicide the victim has identified himself with the hated other person. Unconsciously, he fantasizes committing his deadly act on that other person. The process of identification, so often involved in the defense mechanism of turning against the self, will be considered more fully in Chapter 3.

Definition

Turning against the self is the automatic and unconscious process through which a person deflects hostile aggression from another person and directs it onto himself. By this means the identity of the original object of the hostility remains obscure, and sometimes the emotion of hostility itself remains outside of conscious awareness. When hostility is turned inward on the self, the person may injure himself physically or in other ways—socially, financially, and the like.

Clinical Examples

Example 1. A young homosexual woman, strongly attached to an older partner, was deeply hurt and disappointed when her partner was unfaithful. On learning of the infidelity, the patient slashed her own wrists. She experienced no physical pain but noted a tremendous feeling of relief as soon as she began to slash herself. In the course of psychoanalytic psychotherapy she discovered that in her relationship with her partner she was expressing the unconscious need of an infant for its mother. The act of infidelity threatened her with abandonment, and made her feel like an angry infant who can only express rage on her own body. By hurting herself, she, in fact, hurt her partner by causing her to experience guilt and remorse similar to that which a mother suffers when her child is injured because of the mother's neglect.

Example 2. A young schizophrenic patient yearned for a special dictionary as a birthday present from her mother. Instead, the mother sent her a set of ornate dinner plates, although the mother knew that her daughter loathed such domestic articles. On receiving the gift, the patient felt intense rage and a strong urge to smash the plates. Instead, she carefully put them away on an upper shelf of a closet, safe from harm. Later that day she made a serious suicide attempt, thus turning her destructive rage against herself. This act of self-destruction was, she said, a wish to destroy "the part of me that is my mother—the mother inside of me." Like the mother, the daughter had become exceedingly obese, destroying her considerable youthful beauty as she came to look more and more like her portly mother whom she hated and despised, but from whom she also yearned for love and affection.

Example 3. A 50-year-old female patient who lived with her 30-year-old unmarried son described an incident of the preceding day when she had developed an upper respiratory infection and fever. Her son, who had a social engagement for the evening, inquired whether she would be all right if he went out. She cheerfully replied, "Of course I'll be all right! Don't worry!"

After her son's departure, she went to bed feeling abandoned and lonely, but not in the least consciously resentful. As her self-pity increased, she experienced a mounting, unreasonable worry for her son's safety. Clad only in a thin gown, she got out of bed to watch anxiously from a window for her son's return. Although the house became very cold, she did not readjust the thermostat. When her son returned at 2 o'clock in the morning, she was having violent fits of coughing and was trembling with the cold. Her son was obviously angry when he saw his mother's plight, and she apologetically explained to him, "I was worried about you, so I decided to stay up and wait for you." With this comment, the son's anger erupted, and he berated his mother for getting out of bed, for sitting in a cold house, and for not clothing herself warmly. She experienced a sense of deep satisfaction at her son's outburst, and realized that she had upset him greatly. This gave her a sense of victory and control. She was quite unmindful that she had suffered several hours of extreme discomfort and had actually jeopardized her health to achieve this Pyrrhic victory. Her anger and resentment at her son was completely unconscious, and had been turned against herself.

Example 4. A gently cynical, wryly humorous professor of English literature suffered from a middle life depression. In describing his profound feelings of unworthiness and sense of past sinfulness, he was reminded of the poem "Once in a Saintly Passion" by the British poet James Thomson (1834–1882).

Once in a saintly passion
I cried with desperate grief,
"Oh Lord, my heart is black with guile,
Of sinners I am Chief."

Then stooped my Guardian Angel
And whispered from behind,
"Vanity, my little man,
You're nothing of the kind."

After reciting the poem, the patient reported that in the past he had actually felt like the world's greatest sinner and most unworthy person, but that it had suddenly dawned on him that this was a rather grandiose and exalted position to assume. After this realization, he became aware of a generalized anger "toward the whole world," because his considerable talents had not been acclaimed sufficiently. On achieving this insight, he observed a distinct lessening of his depression, became more realistically assertive, and ceased to minimize and disclaim his considerable talent. He no longer turned his anger against himself in the form of extreme self-condemnation.

Clinical Syndromes Which Illustrate Turning Against the Self

Clinical syndromes or life circumstances in which turning against the self may be most clearly observed are twofold. First, the young child who is hospitalized for a protracted period often bites and scratches himself and bangs his head as an expression of his anger. Such behavior is an early analogue of the mechanism of turning against the self. The child's rage is actually meant for the parent who he feels has abandoned him and exposed him to pain and loneliness. Characteristically, this anger is directly expressed toward the parent when the child returns home.

Second, people who have attempted suicide often describe vividly the relief from tension which results when they take this action. Some also become aware that the act involves a wish to hurt someone else with whom they are identified. Suicide, of course, remains the ultimate form of turning against the self. With the exception of rationally motivated suicide, as in a person dying from an incurable and painful disease, some authorities say that every suicide is an unconsciously intended murder.

Occurrence of Turning against the Self in Normal Behavior

When enraged but helpless to vent their impulses against others, small children often fall to the floor, screaming and kicking with such vigor as to hurt themselves. In more extreme instances they will smash their own valued possessions, or hurt themselves in other ways. In moments of great frustration, mature adults also will strike their own heads as they berate themselves verbally with such comments as, "I am so stupid. How could I have done such a thing?" Or they will bang a fist on a table or wall so hard as to bruise or cause pain.

DISSOCIATION

General Comments

Cases of multiple personality most clearly exemplify dissociation. In this condition, a person has one or more auxilliary sets of organized personality traits which are repressed and hidden from himself and the world. Episodically, the second (or third, fourth, etc.) set of personality traits abruptly replaces the person's usual characteristics. These episodes may last minutes, hours, days, or longer during which time the repressed personality traits take command and the person acts as if he were another person whose character traits are grossly different from those he ordinarily exhibits. The phenomenon of the mild and pleasant man who becomes belligerent after a few drinks is similar to dissociation. The story of Dr. Jekyll and Mr. Hyde, a fictional account of two complete and totally opposite personalities which alternated in one person, may readily be construed as an example of dissociation.

The behaviors that occur during dissociation are later repressed, and the person is left with no memory for what he did or how he felt during the episode. Thus, his normal personality is spared any knowledge of his other self. When dissociated pathological motives achieve the complexity of a complete second personality, that second personality usually goes by a different name, as did Mr. Hyde. In less extensive instances of dissociation, the person simply behaves in some unusual way for which he is amnesic. A dramatic example of a very complicated case of multiple personality is described by Thigpen and Cleckley (1957) in their book *The Three Faces of Eve.* Recently a report on an even more complicated case was published by Schreiber (1973) in the book *Sybil,* an account of a girl who at various times had 16 different personalities, including 2 who were male.

Definition

Dissociation is the involuntary process through which a person's mental functions are split or divided in a manner which allows him to express forbidden and ordinarily unconscious impulses without his having any sense of responsibility for his actions—either because he later is unable to remember his disowned behavior or because he does not experience it as being his own at the time it occurs. Such behavior is different from and usually at odds with the patient's ordinary standards of conduct, and is not characteristic for that person in his usual state of consciousness.

Clinical Examples

Example 1. The case of the 42-year-old housewife who regressed to infantile speech and behavior (described in the section on regression, p. 76), also illustrates dissociation. This patient had episodes in which a childlike personality organization emerged, causing her to behave in an infantile manner completely different from her ordinary personality. On termination of the episode, she became amnesic for the period in which her disowned child-self was in control of her thoughts and behavior. In this example, we see the overlap and interplay of various mechanisms of defense. Ordinarily, this woman coped with her underlying childlike self through repression, thus keeping it out of awareness. When repression failed, there was an eruption of the childlike, conflict-producing motivational patterns and personality organization. When repression was re-instituted, the infantile behavior and motivations were again represssed, whereupon she became amnesic for the events which occurred during the period of domination by infantile personality traits.

Example 2. A 33-year-old woman suffered from profound feelings of apathy after a divorce which had been as devastating and chaotic as her preceding 5 years of marriage. She found it difficult to initiate any sort of activity, even ordinary household tasks. She spent most of her time sitting immobile, staring into space, enveloped by feelings of indifference. After several weeks of suffering in this manner, she was able to muster enough initiative to seek psychiatric treatment.

During the course of psychoanalytic psychotherapy, she began to feel intense rage toward her brutal, sadistic, and psychotic ex-husband. As she increasingly experienced these rageful feelings, she became very anxious. During one treatment session, while in the throes of an anxiety attack, she suddenly became quite calm and reported that she was now situated on the ceiling in a far corner of the office. From this distant vantage point, she was blandly observing the person lying on the couch. She could recognize the person on the couch as an aspect of herself, but the self on the ceiling experienced none of the violent emotion which the other one on the couch possessed. For several weeks, whenever she was threatened with the emergence of her rageful and murderous impulses during an analytic session, she automatically split off this unacceptable enraged aspect of herself and viewed it from the distant corner as if it were some scientific specimen. Gradually she became more acquainted with her rage and began to integrate it and acknowledge it as part of herself. Only then could she reunite the two aspects of herself—the enraged self lying on the couch, and the calm, observing self who watched from a distant corner of the room.

Example 3. A 36-year-old mother of four children sought treatment ostensibly for her inability to get along well with her husband. He complained incessantly about her "stupidity and ineptness." She admitted that he had good reason for his complaints, but she also realized that she exhibited these traits only in his presence. With other people, she behaved quite differently. When not in her husband's presence she participated actively in the extracurricular functions of the private school in which her children were enrolled where she showed herself to be original and artistically creative. She took advanced courses in philosophy at a local university where she distinguished herself scholastically. She worked diligently and productively in several community organizations, and she carried on an active and rewarding social life by herself when her husband was on his frequent trips out of town.

Her difficulty revolved around a strange transformation which overtook her in late afternoon just before the hour when her husband was to come home. At that time her thinking became foggy, her capacity for planning diminished, and her coordination and motor skills deteriorated. She became clumsy and broke dishes and damaged furniture—her entire demeanor became stodgy and sullen. The observing part of herself made her aware of this dramatic transformation, but she was powerless to influence it. As soon as her husband arrived home she burned food, spilled drinks, made stupid conversation, and, in general, by her own admission, became "an inept and revolting slob."

She never lost the power to observe this inept self and was sufficiently concerned about her lack of control over it to seek psychiatric help. After many months of treatment, she was able to come to grips with her rage toward her husband whom she felt to be cold, isolated, aloof, demanding, and exacting. She came to understand that her strange transformation into the "inept and revolting slob" was an involuntary expression of her resentment and anger toward her husband. When she overcame her childlike fear of his critical and disapproving demeanor and was able to be more realistically assertive, her own sabotaging behavior which seemed to have a life of its own, diminished.

Example 4. The patient described by Thigpen and Cleckley (1957) in their book *The Three Faces of Eve* is a notable example of a woman who had three distinct personalities each of which existed without the knowledge of the other two. Frazier and Carr (1964) describe another dramatic case of multiple personality. In her usual personality, a patient, Martha, was a very conscientious mother and wife who was given to periods of suicidal depression. In her other personality she went by the name of Stella. Stella was a loud, profane woman who drank heavily and was sexually promiscuous. As Stella, the patient knew of the existence of Martha, but when the Martha personality was in control, she had no knowledge of the immoral Stella.

Clinical Syndromes Which Illustrate Dissociation

Clinical syndromes of life circumstances in which dissociation may be observed include fugue states and episodes of amnesia, hysterial neuroses, dissociative type (formerly called dissociative reactions), and cases of multiple personality.

Also the sense of calm and pleasurable detachment experienced by many people at the moment that their death seemed imminent and inescapable. Noyes (1972) has cited numerous examples, such as mountain climbers who fell hundreds of feet but were not killed. As they fell, they felt calm, blissful, and even ecstatic, and some heard beautiful, heavenly music during what they thought were the last seconds of their lives. And finally, the "morning after" syndrome in which one's behavior while drunk the previous evening is not remembered clearly. As the mental fog lifts and the person begins to remember his actions, he may feel great shame and remorse if he had, in fact, behaved inappropriately the night before.

Occurrence of Dissociation in Normal Behavior

Severe and uncontrollable dissociation does not occur in normal people except under conditions of extreme stress. It may then appear transiently in an otherwise reasonably well-integrated person. Stuart Miller (1962) has cited a number of fascinating examples of lifesaving instances of dissociative episodes in prisoners being mercilessly grilled by the Gestapo. One such prisoner described in the section on regression (p. 75), after standing for long hours with his nose pressed to the wall of a stinking cellar while being interrogated, suddenly began to see (and believe himself to be in) a lovely garden on a beautiful island. Many survivors of Nazi prisons have reported such experiences. The phenomenon was sufficiently well known among the involuntary guests of the Gestapo that they coined the term, "The cinema of the prisoners."

The reader may well question our use of the case of the prisoner of the Nazis to illustrate both regression and dissociation. This question points again to the issue of the kinship and intertwining of various mechanisms of defense. In dissociation, there is an interplay among several mechanisms. Repression fails, and the person then regresses to an earlier mode of mental activity which allows wishes to be gratified magically, as in the instance of the prisoner. In the more psychopathologic cases of dissociation, regression permits an earlier mode of mental activity which allows children to split their sense of self into a good self and a bad self (see Chapter 1 and the section on identification in Chapter 3). In dissociation the bad self directs behavior which overtly expresses forbidden impulses. When these impulses have again succumbed to repression, the bad self and the forbidden impulses are again relegated in the psyche's underground. The good self regains control of behavior but, because of repression, is spared knowledge of the forbidden behavior that occurred. This brief resume is, of course, a highly oversimplified account of very complex mental events.

These more extreme examples of dissociation are similar to the intense fantasies in adults which Thurber (1947) described so delightfully in *The Secret Life of Walter Mitty*. During such regressive moments of absorption in fantasy, the adult, like the child engrossed in play, does not just think he is a soldier or a nurse, but temporarily he *is* the soldier or the nurse. Such fantasy experiences are also similar to the experience many actors have while performing in a play. If the actor fully immerses himself in the part, while on stage he *is* the character he portrays. At times, actors experience some difficulty in getting out of the role, and their behavior in real life continues in some measure to be that of the character in the play.

Fantasy in normal people, then, is qualitatively similar to the phenomenon of multiple personalities or the outbursts of less well-organized behavior in fugue states, in which infantile unconscious motivations seize control and are expressed overtly. The outburst may then be repressed with resulting amnesia. In normal fantasy, the relatively forbidden impulses are expressed only in thought, a form of behavior that represents trial action in imagination. Fantasy in the normal person is under better conscious control, and can be stopped when the person desires—except, of course, in the instance of night dreams. Nightmares express fearsome unconscious impulses which, in a disguised form have been able to escape the controlling vigilance of the Ego and emerge as fantasies in the sleeping state, often provoking sufficient anxiety to awaken the dreamer and put a stop to the fantasy.

REFERENCES

Brenner C: An Elementary Textbook of Psychoanalysis, (ed 2). New York, International Universities, 1973
Fraiberg SH: The Magic Years. New York, Scribner's, 1959
Frazier SH, Carr AC: Introduction to Psychopathology. New York, MacMillan, 1964
Freedman AM, Kaplan HI (eds): Comprehensive Textbook of Psychiatry. Baltimore, Williams & Wilkins, 1967
Freud A: The Ego and Mechanisms of Defense. New York, International Universities, 1946
Freud S: The psychopathology of everyday life. Standard Edition, vol 6. London, Hogarth, 1960
Freud S: Analysis of a phobia in a five-year-old boy. Standard Edition, vol 10. London, Hogarth, 1955a
Freud S: Notes upon a case of obsessional neurosis. Standard Edition, vol 10. London, Hogarth, 1955b
Kolb LD: Modern Clinical Psychiatry (ed 8). Philadelphia, Saunders, 1973
Kris E: Psychoanalytic Explorations in Art. New York, International Universities, 1952
Menninger K: Man Against Himself. New York, Harcourt Brace, 1938
Miller SC: Ego-Autonomy in sensory deprivation, isolation, and stress. Int J Psychoanal 43:1-20, 1962
Noyes R: The experience of dying. Psychiatry 35:174-184, 1972
Schreiber FR: Sybil. Chicago, Henry Regnery, 1973
Thigpen, CH, Cleckley HM: The Three Faces of Eve. New York, McGraw-Hill, 1957
Thurber J: The secret life of walter mitty, in Kielty B (ed): A Treasury of Short Stories. New York, Simon & Schuster, 1947
Wolf SG, Goodell H: Behavioral Science in Clinical Medicine. Springfield, Ill; Thomas, 1975

3

Identification, Sublimation, and Compensation: Mental Processes Sometimes Used as Defenses

The three mental processes, identification, sublimation, and compensation, are essential to normal personality development, but under certain circumstances, they may also serve as mechanisms of defense. As mechanisms of defense, they have the same function as those mechanisms described in Chapter 2, that is, they are used automatically and unconsciously to lessen anxiety and diminish conflict which threatens to overwhelm the Ego and impair its functioning. In this chapter we shall examine identification, sublimation, and compensation as they are used in the service of defense.

IDENTIFICATION

General Comments

The term *identification*, when used to designate a mechanism of defense, refers to one aspect of the universal, automatic, and unconscious tendency of the human being to internalize[1] various parts

---

[1]Other important mental activities involved in the process of internalization are incorporation and introjection. We choose deliberately to omit discussion of introjection and incorporation for the sake of clarity and in the interest of avoiding a confusing issue. We acknowledge the risks involved in too much elision, but still view it as the preferred course. We refer readers interested in pursuing the topic further to the monograph by Schafer (1968) in which he discusses this problem in detail.

of the environment. The environment is internalized in different ways. Physical objects may be ingested through the mouth. Objects, including people, may be psychologically ingested through the sense organs and become internalized as mental representations in memory. When a person is internalized in this manner, his emotional attributes (real and imagined) as well as his physical appearance becomes part of the mental representation of him. The store of such mental representations of emotionally important people play a crucial role in normal behavior.

For example, a daughter who is planning to marry may anticipate in a daydream how she will introduce her fiance to her parents. In fantasy, she conjures up the memories of fiance, mother, and father as she imagines how the discussion will proceed when she introduces her fiance to her parents. The internalized images of mother, father, and fiance hold a complicated conversation in her thoughts. According to the outcome of the conversation, the young woman may change her plan for informing her parents of her intentions, and decide to invite her fiance to her home several times before telling her parents of her plans. She is able to predict with reasonable accuracy how parents and fiance will actually behave because she can visualize how the internalized representations of them behave in various situations.

To the extent that such memory images of people are accurate representations of them, these mental representations help to organize behavior along realistic lines. However, the internalized representations of people who are important in a person's current life tend to merge and combine with childishly unrealistic mental images of people who were important in earlier times—especially the parents.

Children, because their thinking is characterized by animism, egocentricity, concreteness, and omnipotence, develop unrealistic and contradictory mental images of their parents which are not consistent with the parent's actual behavior. They tend to split the images of childhood figures into good (all-loving and adoring) and bad (always hostile, dangerous, derogating) images. When the representations of people in current life become too much merged or tinged with either the unrealistically good or the bad parental representations, contemporary people are perceived as having irrationally good or irrationally bad attributes.

This confusion was illustrated by a college student who became indignant in the course of a discussion with a professor over a grade the student received on an examination. The student's mental representation of the professor, who in actuality was a mild-mannered man but an exacting teacher, had become merged with and, so to speak, contaminated by the student's mental representation developed in childhood of his mild-mannered and exceedingly indulgent father. Throughout the student's life his father had treated him as if he were a royal prince who could do no wrong and who always deserved special consideration. Because the image of the teacher was merged with that of the indulgent father who never held his son to exacting standards, the student automatically assumed that the professor possessed attitudes identical with those of his father. When the actual behavior of the teacher violated the order of the student's universe, the student was surprised, bewildered, and angered by the teacher's strict grading. The influence of his inner representation of his indulgent father profoundly distorted both his perceptions and his judgment, and led him to expect unrealistically indulgent treatment from other people who occupy quasi-parental roles.

The ultimate fate of what has been "internalized" varies: in the case of objects taken into the mouth, they may be either swallowed or spit out. If swallowed, they may be digested and become assimilated as an integral part of the body. We can construct a psychological counterpart for this process. The psychological representation of an external object (person or thing) may be taken in, psychologically "mouthed," and then rejected ("spit out"); this is analogous to the mechanism of projection. Or, an object may be internalized and not rejected; that is, it may be psychologically "swallowed," in which case it may then be psychologically "digested" and become assimilated as an integrated part of the personality. Through this last process, in one or more aspects of thought, feeling, or behavior, the person psychologically internalizes other people and becomes similar to them in some aspects of his mode of thought, feeling, or behavior. We refer to this as *identification* with the person.

Identification is of particular significance in very early life, and as a generalization, one may say that the tendency to identify bears a direct relationship to the stage of primitiveness of Ego development; that is, the earlier the stage of Ego development, the greater the use of identification. The earliest identification, often referred to as *primary* identification, is that of the infant with the mother, who is the first and most important person in the infant's life. It is through her that he receives gratification for his basic needs for food, love, warmth, comfort, stimulation, and other needs. On the basis of experimental observations on the interactions between mothers and their infants and the data from the psychoanalytic treatment of adults, we have reason to believe that during this very early stage of development the human infant cannot distinguish between himself and his mother. When the mother is warm, loving, and relaxed in her interactions with the baby, he feels good as she does. When she is angry or upset and tense in her interactions with him, he feels bad. Because of his inability to distinguish between himself and his mother, these experiences during which he feels like the mother constitute a totalistic identification with her. In the early months of life he thus identifies with her, becomes like her.

The dramatic consequences of a failure to advance beyond this stage of primary identification with the mother can be observed in the clinical syndrome of male transsexualism. When a male infant is reared by a mother who forms a certain kind of extremely close and intense relationship with her infant son, the little boy develops an irreversible and totalistic identification with her. As the studies by Stoller (1968, 1974), Green (1974) and others have shown, this kind of early identification with the mother produces the clinical condition of male transsexualism. Transsexuals are physically normal males who grow into adulthood with a profound sense of being feminine in all of their needs, sexual desires, and emotions. Such a man looks and behaves like a woman because he has never relinquished his primary identification with his mother.

Normally, the infant relinquishes his early, totalistic primary identification with his mother. He progressively forms other attachments, and identifies with various attributes of both of his parents as well as other people in the family. Emergence from the infantile stage of primary identification with the mother is characterized by imitative behavior, as seen in such activities as smiling, gesturing, and game playing. Those who have observed a child learning to talk must be impressed by the imitation involved in the effort to duplicate the speech of parents and older siblings, illustrating the important roles that imitation and identification play in speech development. The same may be observed in the acquisition of mannerisms, ideals, interests, hobbies, and styles of thought. By the same token, adaptive and defensive reaction patterns are also often derived from identification with the parents, an important factor in determining the choice of mechanisms of defense which a given person will make, a complex issue which we discuss further in Chapter 6. Children of both sexes initially identify with the mother. Later they begin to imitate and identify with other people and develop secondary identifications. This process is most clearly observed in the way the boy child very early turns toward some important male in his environment, usually his father, but sometimes an older brother, uncle, or other adult male as the process of secondary identification with men supersedes the primary identification with the mother.

After sufficient psychic development has occurred for the child to be able to distinguish himself from others, clear-cut secondary identifications become evident. This later secondary type of identification is seen in the way that children resolve their anxiety-laden Oedipal rivalry by identification with the parent of the same sex. This process is most clearly observable in the little boy's identification with his father. His hatred of his father and his wish to replace him in the affections of his mother produce unbearable anxiety, because the child becomes terrified at the thought that his father will retaliate in some dreadful manner. In addition, the boy child feels guilt over his hatred for his father because he also loves and needs him. He resolves his dilemma by relinquishing his rivalry, and in its stead he identifies with his father, "I do not hate you; I want to be like you." This identification strengthens the little boy's sense of masculinity and consolidates a friendly and admiring relationship to his father. It also helps to organize his voice of conscience. The girl's relation to her mother performs a similar function.

Although the child normally identifies predominantly with the parent of the same sex, there are always partial identifications with the other parent. This accounts for the admixture of masculine and feminine traits and characteristics which can be observed in any of us, since the result of identification is to become like the other person—to be the same, fulfill his role, and learn to perform his functions. The importance of this process of identification for the maintenance of relationships to other people can readily be appreciated, but the special importance which it has for the developing child must be stressed. The child's character is shaped by his identifications with parents and other people who are important figures during his earliest years; through such identifications he accepts and assimilates their values, beliefs, and patterns of behavior. But this tendency to identify with an important person is by no means limited to early childhood; it is also an important process in adolescence when persons in this age range affect the dress, speech, mannerisms, and hair styles of admired heroes of stage, screen or gridiron. Although these adolescent identifications are often transient, many are enduring and important; for example, teachers of adolescents often become much more than just teachers—they become models whose influence remains for years, sometimes for a lifetime.

During the adolescent stage of development, the young person must remold his collection of identifications with people who were important to him during childhood as well as his identifications with current figures; he must now recast these various identifications into an identity uniquely his own. Until the adolescent is able to establish coherence and unity among his earlier identifications, he often appears to be an unpredictable and awkward collection of parts that do not fit together well. For example, the young adolescent boy may walk with the exaggerated swagger of a cowboy as he leaves a movie in which his current Hollywood hero has won the West. He has not, in any coherent or integrated fashion, become like the screen character, nor has this partial attribute of the movie hero yet become a natural and integrated aspect of the young person's manner of walking. The same boy may have his hair cut like a favorite teacher, dress like an older friend who is a football hero, talk in a fashion reminiscent of his father, and have a temper like his mother. To the observer he seems to be an awkward collection of parts changeable without notice and not yet unified as a person in his own right. As Erikson (1959, 1963) has emphasized, the developmental task which the adolescent faces involves the unification and organization of these various and disparate identifications into an enduring, coherent, integrated identity of his own. When things go well, the adolescent emerges from this chaotic period with a stable sense of who he is and what he hopes to become as he develops his own identity by synthesizing current and earlier childhood identifications into an entity uniquely his own. In later life, the processes of identification tend to be less obvious and less easily discerned than they are in childhood and adolescence. The adult is not likely to recognize or acknowledge his identification with someone whom he admires; he tends to be unaware when he purchases his clothing from the same haberdasher as that of his boss, or drives the same model car as his favorite athlete.

֣ The tendency to be like someone admired is familiar and seems understandable; however both adults and children tend also to identify with people whom they fear and even hate when such people are in a position of power. Anna Freud (1946) originally called our attention to this type of identification in her monograph *The Ego and the Mechanisms of Defense.* She describes how children cope with a threatening person by identifying with that person. In this manner he transforms himself from a frightened child into a person who frightens others. Through this "identification with the aggressor," the child masters anxiety. Although internalization is a universal human attribute, and is involved to some degree in all relations with other people, under certain conditions the process can also serve the purposes of defense. For example, the child who is hurt and afraid of sudden temper outbursts from an otherwise loving mother, or by a painful visit to the dentist, may cope with the rage, fear, and helplessness stirred in him by these experiences by identifying with the person he fears. He can be observed for some days after such a traumatic experience to shout angrily at his doll or his dog or his little sister, as his mother had shouted at him—or he will be the frightening dentist treating the doll, the dog, or the little sister. In such situations of real or fantasied threat from another person, the child avoids anxiety and helplessness by "saying" to himself (not consciously, of course) "I fear you but if I become like you, I will be as powerful as you and no longer will need to be afraid; indeed, I can frighten others as you frighten me."

This type of identification is an important early component in the formation of the Superego; the child identifies with parental threats of punishment, thereby warding off the threat of punishment from the outside through identifying with the source of that threat. The parental voice of discipline is now organized as an internal voice of conscience. In these instances, we can see the gradual shading and insensible merging of the use of identification as a developmental process with its use as a defensive process. Although the process of identification routinely plays a crucial role in normal personality development, we have included it in this special section because, at times, it may also be used as a defense. Let us now consider the conditions under which it is used unequivocally as a defense mechanism, aside from those other purposes it fulfills in normal development. Identification as a defense mechanism is most clearly exemplified in two situations, identification with the aggressor and identification with a lost object.

Identification with the aggressor refers to the automatic and unconscious process through which a person avoids anxiety by becoming like a feared aggressive person, or (especially in children) becoming like a feared animal or thing. The awesome and frightening power of the feared person is then perceived as though it emanates from one's self, is under one's own control, and may be directed toward others.

Identification with a lost object refers to the automatic and unconscious process through which a person defends himself against anxiety and grief resulting from the loss of an emotionally important person by identifying with the lost person. By means of identification he becomes like the lost person and thereby symbolically retains the relationship. He feels, "I have not lost him because I am him—I therefore have him with me."

It should now be evident that identification is a complex mechanism, and also that it is universally used in normal personality development and, at times, as a defense. Through this complicated process of psychological internalization, the child assimilates the standards of his parents so that they become part of his own personality—his own ideals and guidelines which discipline his behavior even when his parents are absent. Many conflicts are resolved through identification; but in addition to the resolution of conflict, identification is also commonly used to alleviate the pain of loss which occurs under many ordinary circumstances of life, as we sometimes see in the course of mourning, when the person adopts characteristics, attitudes, or mannerisms of the deceased, even though such characteristics may formerly have been alien to the personality of the grieving person. Identification as a defense against grief is quite common, and in some instances will produce physical symptoms in the bereaved which are similar to the symptoms suffered by the dead person during his fatal illness. Thus, the bereaved avoids or lessens his sense of loss by holding on, psychologically speaking, to the image of the lost person. Such loss may occur by death, desertion, or from the waning of love or friendship of another person. One can also lose a fantasied relationship; for instance, a shy young man may form an intense fantasy love relation with a young woman to whom he never speaks. In his fantasies she is the most perfect person imaginable. If he actually meets her, perhaps even marries her, and then finds to his distress that she falls far short of his idealized fantasy of her, he suffers a very serious psychological loss although the actual relationship with her continues.

Definition

Identification, when used as a defense, refers to the automatic and unconscious assumption of traits, qualities, and characteristics of some emotionally important person to avoid or lessen conflict which stems either from the real or the symbolic loss of that person or from fear of real or fantasied aggression by that person.

Clinical Examples

Example 1. A 45-year-old physician became acutely depressed immediately on learning of the death by suicide of his 80-year-old mother. The mother had been a childlike, selfish, and totally egocentric person all her life. To a degree, her son realized that his mother had these unpleasant attributes, but for years he had also insisted that she was not as unpleasant as everyone else knew her to be.

At the funeral he was preoccupied with the thought, "I see the casket but mother isn't really inside. She isn't really gone." As he became depressed, he began to sit for long hours with a sullen look on his face, sigh periodically, hold his hands above his head in a beseeching motion, and grind his teeth. He talked only of how bad he felt and refused to attend to any obligation "because he was too fatigued." Because he was unable to work, he sought psychiatric help. In discussing the history of her husband's illness, his wife stated that he had become "like a different person." As she described his strange posture, hand gestures, teeth grinding, and preoccupation with fatigue, she suddenly realized that he was acting exactly as his mother had for years. She stated, "It's just like his mother had come to live with us."

As treatment progressed, the patient came to realize how tenaciously he was holding on to the memory of the dead mother by becoming like her. He had never unpacked or even opened the chest containing her personal possessions and clothing which she had willed to him. When he finally brought himself to open the chest and give away the clothing, he commented, "Now I feel she is really gone." With this acceptance of the actuality of the mother's death, his symptoms, which were the obvious result of identification with her, gradually disappeared. In their stead, he felt both grief at her death and anger at the real hurt and difficulty she had caused him over the years. The identification spared him awareness of both his childlike attachment to his mother and his infantile rage at her.

Example 2. Bruno Bettleheim (1943) observed a remarkable and widespread tendency among Jews in Nazi concentration camps to identify with their Nazi guards as a defense against helpless terror of their captors. Although these prisoners hated all that the Nazis represented, after a time they tended to adopt the brusque manner and military walk of their guards, borrowed and bought articles of Nazi uniform to wear, and coerced other prisoners just as the Nazi guards did. These prisoners became unofficial assistant guards often called on by the Nazis to help discipline other inmates. This, of course, is another example of what Anna Freud has designated as identification with the aggressor.

Example 3. The 18-year-old daughter of a famous and flamboyant attorney known throughout the world for his capacity to charm a jury and hold an audience, was admitted to a psychiatric hospital after committing a series of dramatic delinquent acts at the school in which she was enrolled. Some of her delinquencies were performed in the nude, thus attracting a large audience of fellow students, newspaper reporters, policemen, and others. In the hospital, she continued to enact dramatic delinquencies. These childish and regressive acts caricatured the spellbinding and exhibitionistic performance of her famous father whom she deeply loved but also bitterly resented because he seemed to have greater concern for his clients than for his family and to be more interested in getting press notices than in the welfare of his daughter. This identification with the father was a way of feeling closer to him while simultaneously mocking and punishing him by making a travesty of his spectacular performances.

Clinical Syndromes Which Illustrate Identification

Since identification is prominent in early stages of personality development, any psychological disturbance which involves a significant amount of regression revives the early identifications with other people who were emotionally significant in childhood. Consequently, one can see identification operating in bold relief in a variety of severe psychiatric illnesses. Among them are

1. Severe depressive, schizophrenic, and other regressive states
2. Conditions of extreme loss as in grief
3. Conditions in which a person is subjected to extreme aggression
4. Conversion reactions in which the patient's paralysis, anesthesia, or other bodily dysfunction is often modeled on similar physical disturbances in other people important to the patient, particularly people important in his childhood
5. Fugue states and multiple personalities. In states of multiple personality, the repressed and disowned personality (or personalities) which from time-to-time seizes control of consciousness and overt behavior is often constructed from identifications with other people. When this other personality emerges, the person acts as if he were someone quite different from his usual self.

Occurrence of Identification in Normal Behavior

Beginning with the imitation of adult sounds, gestures, and facial expressions by infants, the human being has a lifelong tendency to internalize the attributes of others who are important to him, and to integrate these internalized attributes more or less smoothly into his own personality. Such internalizations form the basic building blocks for the growth of a healthy personality in childhood, but they may also constitute some of the most important causes of pathologic personality development.

To the extent that parents and teachers are loving but not overly indulgent in their care; firm but not crushing in their discipline; optimistic but not excessive in their expectations; and attentive to but not unduly preoccupied with the child, identification with them will provide sound material for personality formation. Parallel to the development of such healthy mental representations of others, the child will develop a healthy mental representation of himself from what Harry Stack Sullivan (1947) has so aptly called the "reflected appraisals" of significant others.

Just as the mental representations of significant others, especially the parents, may be split into good and bad images, the self-representation built initially from the reflected appraisal of others may be split into representations of an unrealistically good (lovable, omnipotent) self and an unrealistically bad (evil, destructive, contemptible) self. We saw how such unrealistically good and bad self-representations may at times usurp consciousness and control behavior in the instance of the multiple personalities described in *The Three Faces of Eve* or in Sybil's reported 16 different selves.

An important critical point in personality development occurs during the period of 4 to 6 years of age when the child uses identification to resolve his fantasy-ridden Oedipal competitiveness and love attachments. As a result of identification with the parents, especially with the parent of the same sex, the approving and disapproving attributes and attitudes of the parents now come to reside within the child's personality as the Superego. With the establishment of the Superego, the child's self-representation is increasingly molded from within and becomes, therefore, progressively less dependent on the reflected appraisal of others for its further development.

At adolescence, the primitive childhood mental representations of self and others, so frequently split in early childhood into irrationally good and bad aspects, are reorganized and integrated into a sense of identity as a person unique and separate from others and into a more reasonable and realistic Superego.

Even after such integration, in moments of significant loss as in grief, the adult defends himself from the threat that loss imposes by reverting for a time to identification with the lost person. Similarly, in conditions involving severe disruption of psychological integration, especially psychotic states, we see the fragmentation of personality into the various identifications from which it originally was formed. The bad and threatening aspects of such internalizations tend under these conditions to be further defended against by projection.

Transient and reversible identification with others is the basis for tact, empathy, and the capacity to understand how others feel—to put one's self in the other person's shoes, as the saying goes. In this instance, identification is not blindly compelled by the necessity to avoid conflict over unwanted unconscious impulses, but it is, nonetheless, in great measure automatic and involuntary.

Conflict over unconscious impulses may produce two opposite disturbances of empathy. When impulses are too rigidly defended against, the person can neither sense such urges and emotions in himself nor similar urges and emotions in other people. He will be devoid of empathy in regard to those specific emotions, and hence tactless and insensitive in dealing with others who exhibit them. At the other extreme, people who are unduly motivated by unconscious, infantile needs tend to lose perspective and "over identify" with others who have similar needs. Over identification occurs frequently among adolescents as they attempt to fight against the unduly harsh dictates of the infantile aspects of their own consciences. Some adolescents identify passionately with the underdog against the unfair establishment; other adolescents, with equal passion, over identify with the power of the establishment in their hatred of those who challenge its authority. Thus, both the young member of the Ku Klux Klan and the antiestablishment hippie throw themselves into ideological war with a ferocity that betrays that each is as much involved in a struggle with something within himself as he is with an actual social issue.

SUBLIMATION

General Comments

Sublimation is as much related to the expression of instinctual drive as it is to defensive operations of the Ego which oppose the expression of such drives. Although much socially valued behavior is based on sublimation, it does not explain the existence of complex, sophisticated behaviors such as artistic productions and scientific achievements; it only explains some of the motive force behind them. Whether sublimation can be properly regarded as a defense mechanism at all is open to question, since it may simply represent the direct and conflict-free expression of controlled drive energy, rather than a defense against drive discharge. When it is regarded as a defense mechanism, it is conceived to be the most complete, mature, and effective one of all.

Originally, Freud regarded sublimation as a loose conceptualization of many different processes that eventuate in some type of behavior of a higher, more socially valued order. In sublimation, infantile and unconscious impulses are expressed and gratified in a form acceptable to the person and to society. For this to be possible, factors other than infantile impulses must be present: notably, talent and social opportunity to exercise it. Unconscious impulses do not create talent, but they can activate talent when it is present. The exercise of such talent permits a partial gratification of the unconscious drive, only now in a conflict-free, disciplined, and socially acceptable form. Since some considerable degree of gratification of instinctual drive is achieved through the use of sublimation, as a defense mechanism it is the most stable and satisfactory of all.

Many patterns of behavior which originated as defenses against conflictual unconscious impulses gradually become fixed attributes of personality, having come to serve needs and possess values independent of their function as defenses against the original conflict. Such autonomous attitudes and behaviors may also serve important needs of society as well as the personal needs of the person, so that behavior that originated as defense against unconscious impulses may come to have great usefulness both for the person and for society generally. But for such behavior to represent sublimation, it must partially gratify the original unconscious urge of which it is an expression, and in this sense is different from a defensive operation that attempts to check and deny expression of the original urge. For example, through the defense mechanism of reaction formation, a primitive, childish urge to smear feces may be replaced by an opposite and more socially useful trait of orderliness and cleanliness. If it is too extreme, such a defense creates a rigid and constricted person who is unable to tolerate even minor disorder or any freedom of emotional expression. Such defensive traits, with their accompanying loss of freedom of emotional expressiveness, can be contrasted with an example of sublimation, that is, with the channeling of such primitive aggressive or sexual urges into gratifying and useful outlets. Let us consider another possible outcome for the above-cited example: if the primitive urge to smear feces occurs in a person with artistic talent and becomes channeled into the artistic outlet of painting, the freedom to be emotionally expressive is not crippled by the constricting and compulsive orderliness and cleanliness which characterizes a reaction formation. Instead, a playful freedom to express emotionally charged impulses is gradually trained and directed into a socially acceptable form of expression, art.

The channeling of aggression and sadism into the highly sublimated professional activity of the surgeon who inflicts trauma and pain on people for the purpose of helping them is another example of sublimation. Sublimatory behavior obviously extends beyond defense. It involves us in the topic of creativity and of native and acquired talents. We can go no further into these issues than to say that the most effective sublimations probably involve the influence of primitive impulses, of native talent, of discipline and training, of challenging and supportive experience, and of a social setting that values and encourages the activity involved in the sublimation.

Definition

Sublimation refers to the automatic and unconscious process through which primitive, infantile, unconscious impulses are gradually molded and channeled into complex behaviors that are satisfying to the person and valuable to society, while adequately discharging those instinctual drives which in great measure motivate the behavior.

Clinical Examples

When sublimation is successful, the resultant behavior is socially adaptive and the person exhibiting it finds pleasure in expressing the original drive. The defensive function of successful sublimation is, therefore, difficult or impossible to detect, in much the same way that the presence of successful repression is difficult to see. When sublimation begins to fail, however, the underlying infantile impulses become apparent and create conflicts.

Example 1. A 45-year-old unmarried businessman, highly respected and admired in the small community in which he lived, sought treatment because of an overwhelming urge to exhibit his penis to members of the Boy Scout troop of which he was Scoutmaster. For more than 20 years, he had been active in Scouting at local, state, and national levels, and had made a significant and much appreciated contribution to his own community by helping to organize new troops and promote the Boy Scouts of America in all strata of the local society. His enthusiastic pursuit of this project had been a source of pleasure and pride to him, and the enormous gratification which he derived from it more than compensated him for his time and personal effort. In addition to the direct pleasure he experienced in his warm friendships with numerous young men, he also derived great satisfaction and self-esteem from the appreciation shown him by the parents of many of the young males of the community whom he had brought into Scouting.

Approximately 1 year before seeking treatment, he learned that he was being passed over for promotion to a high executive position in his bank, a promotion which he felt he deserved. He was greatly shocked and disappointed, but was able to carry on without displaying his depression and distress to others. Several weeks later, when a member of his Scout troop paid an unexpected visit to his apartment to seek advice on a personal matter, the patient became sexually aroused and was unable to prevent his penis from becoming erect. To his further dismay, he found himself wishing to display his erection to the young man. He felt uncomfortable and embarrassed at this urge, and actively attempted to exclude it from his awareness. A few days later, a similar incident occurred with another young member of his troop, and he noted that the intensity of the urge to exhibit his penis had increased appreciably. Following this, he found himself uncontrollably preoccupied with the wish to show his erect penis to various other members of his troop, and he began to devise schemes to be alone with them so that he might have an opportunity to expose himself. Finally, during the course of one of these encounters, he did, in fact, display his erection to one of the Scouts who seemed to regard it with at least mild curiosity and interest. Encouraged by this, the patient on several subsequent occasions displayed his penis to several other Scouts. After one such incident, the young man who was involved reported the event to his parents, who consulted with several other parents. This group of parents decided that the best interest of all would be served by having a discussion with the Scoutmaster and confronting him with the fact that he seemed to be in need of psychiatric help. This was done, and he readily agreed to see a psychiatrist.

During analytic psychotherapy, the patient discovered that his highly gratifying work with young men was partially an expression of longstanding and profound homosexual wishes which were as unacceptable to him as they were powerful. Through scouting, he had found a means of partial gratification of these wishes, while at the same time deriving a considerable sense of pleasure from the esteem in which he was held because of his efforts. Unfortunately, his scouting activities alone did not provide him with sufficient appreciation and esteem, and when it became evident that his considerable competence and expertise in the banking world would not be adequately rewarded, there was a breakthrough of primitive and infantile need for recognition, appreciation, and admiration. This took the form of the now conscious wish to show his penis to young boys, a wish which stemmed from an early childhood desire to have his younger brother admire his penis. The boys in his Scout troop unconsciously represented this brother. Thus, only the breakdown in a hitherto successful sublimation called attention to the infantile urges which this sublimation had both gratified and defended against for many years.

Example 2. A highly successful, brilliant scientist had a driving and passionate concern for the health problems of the economically deprived, especially the impoverished blacks. His research had won him wide acclaim, and he had risen to a position of considerable influence in a governmental agency responsible for improving the delivery of health care to the underprivileged. In this position his aggressive attempts to implement innovative programs of health care led to numerous battles with reactionary political figures. In time he encountered such strong opposition from them that his program was endangered. At that point he began to have periods of anxiety so intense that he sought psychiatric help.

In the course of his therapy, it became clear that his professional activity, valuable as it was in its own right, was also both a defense against and a mode of expression of intense rage that stemmed from traumatic childhood experiences which had never been completely mastered. The patient was born and reared in a small southern town where his affluent paternal uncle was a powerful political figure. A few years older than the patient's father, the uncle was the town banker. He delighted in harrassing the white men who were debtors to his bank and in tormenting the helpless blacks of the community. The uncle took special pleasure in humiliating the patient's father, a weak and financially unsuccessful man. The uncle also frequently bullied the patient, both physically and emotionally. Helpless to strike back, the patient was doubly enraged on those occasions because his father never came to his defense. When the patient was 6 years old, his uncle, a callous white supremacist, organized a lynch mob and forced the patient to watch as the uncle brutally murdered a helpless black man. Then and there the patient vowed someday to fight against men such as his uncle and to set right the wrongs they do. Much of the dedicated work of this man in adulthood stemmed from that childhood vow. His childhood anger at his uncle was in some measure expressed by his dedicated and usually successful fight against reactionary political leaders who opposed his professional programs. When his opponents began to threaten his efforts and endanger his program to improve the lot of impoverished people, the helpless and wild rage of his childhood threatened to reemerge. Intense anxiety resulted as he became unable to channel primitive rage into the socially approved form of vigorous scientific and administrative work which both accomplished much good and simultaneously expressed his need to defeat and overcome the influence of men such as his uncle.

This man's scientific and administrative efforts are a classic example of the use of sublimation as a defense. The defensive function became apparent only as various reality factors began to interfere with his sublimation and when the unconscious urges that it both expressed and defended against began to create intense conflict and anxiety.

COMPENSATION

General Comments

Just as a man whose leg muscles are crippled by polio develops unusually powerful shoulders from walking on crutches, the person who suffers some psychological deficiency because of unconscious conflicts or acquired or hereditary lack may develop other mental functions to make up for his deficit. The key notion is that through compensation, a person attempts to make up for some defect or lack in himself. When compensation is directed against a psychological deficiency, the deficiency is often the consequence of repression, inhibition, or displacement. For example, conflict over sexual impulses may be repressed. The consequent inability to experience sexual feelings fully may produce a painful sense of sexual inadequacy. This sense of inadequacy may then be defended against by compensatory frantic sexual activity, as in nymphomania or Don Juanism. Alternatively, a person who is inhibited sexually may develop a special interest in the study of sexuality.

When compensation is directed against the restriction of action caused by inhibition or phobic avoidance, the person may develop a special interest and competence in performing the formerly avoided or feared activity. A person with a fear of heights may become a skilled and daring mountain climber. In such instances, compensation is sometimes referred to as a *counterphobic defense.*

Definition

Compensation refers to the automatic and unconscious tendency to develop some physical, mental, or emotional function to an unusual degree to conceal or make up for a deficit. Such deficits may be the result of hereditary or acquired defects, unconscious conflict, or efforts at defense against such conflict.

Clinical Examples

Example 1. A 50-year-old attorney suffered all of his life from an intense, unconscious childlike yearning to be dependent on women and to be loved, protected, and cared for as a favorite child by an adoring mother. Unconsciously, he feared these longings in himself lest they tie him to women with such desperate and needful dependence that he would be totally at their mercy, much as a starving man would be at the mercy of someone who holds out the promise of food. His fear of these repressed infantile longings made him unable to form close and lasting relationships with women. He dimly sensed the presence of his infantile needs and this further threatened his sense of manliness. He attempted to overcome this threat and compensate for his sense of masculine inadequacy by frantic Don Juanism and a tireless and extensive social life.

Example 2. A young man felt a vague sense of masculine inadequacy because of incomplete repression of unconscious homosexual impulses. To compensate for this sense of lack, he developed an intense interest in physical culture and rough contact sports at which he came to excel.

Example 3. The case of "Lemon," previously cited as an example of rationalization (p. 59), may also be used to illustrate compensation. "Lemon" was compelled to buy a new car whenever his old one developed the slightest flaw. He resorted to patent rationalization to justify his frequent purchases of automobiles, complaining regularly that his current car was a "lemon" and using that as his reason for purchasing another. Hence his nickname, "Lemon," given him by fellow members of his country club. His need for flawless and perfect autos represented his unwitting effort to make up for a deep-seated psychological sense of inadequacy which fate cruelly reinforced by imposing on him an unusually small stature. He was only 5'5" tall, and weighed barely 120 pounds. Through his ownership of large, flawless, and powerful autos, he compensated for his sense of inferiority, physical and emotional. His compensatory mania for purchasing new automobiles was then further defended against by the use of rationalization.

Example 4. The remarkable case of Joseph Pujol (1857–1945) who performed at the famous Moulin Rouge in Paris probably qualifies as an instance of compensation. In any event, the story is sufficiently novel that it merits recounting. According to Nohain and Caradec (1967), Joseph Pujol performed to capacity audiences at the Moulin Rouge in the 1890s under the stage name of Le Petomane (The Fart). Le Petomane had the remarkable ability to suck huge quantities of air into his colon, and expel it with such exquisite control that in passing flatus from his distended, air-filled colon he could play musical tunes, imitate the stacatto bark of a machine gun, or duplicate the roar of a huge cannon, to say nothing of his ability to blow out a candle at a distance of a foot or more.

This fantastic control over colon and anal sphincter had not always been a pleasing or welcomed ability. Le Petomane discovered it accidentally as a small boy. He was swimming in the ocean, and, as small boys are wont to do, he ducked his head under water, bending his body forward in the process. To his horror he felt the rush of cold sea water distending his colon to the point of causing a colic such as one experiences when given an enema too rapidly. Frightened, he rushed out of the water, only to find himself helplessly forced to expel large amounts of water from his anus soon after he reached the safety of the beach. Terrified that he had some dreadful malady, he told his mother of his problem. She took him to the family doctor who advised that he restrict himself to playing on the beach and avoid going into the ocean. Some years later, Le Petomane experimented further with this strange talent that his hind parts possessed, and found he could voluntarily inhale either air or water through his anus—and expel them at will. In time, he perfected this capacity, and changed it from the frightening and freakish problem of his childhood to a talent which drew larger audiences to the Moulin Rouge than did the acting ability of Sarah Bernhardt! If this is not a remarkable example of compensation, it is a story that we could not resist including.

Clinical Syndromes Which Illustrate Compensation

Clinical syndromes or life circumstances in which compensation may be observed are as follows.

1. Patients suffering from organic brain disease with loss of memory often compensate for this failing by ingenious procedures to remind themselves when they must do such things as keep appointments, pay bills, and keep track of the whereabouts of possessions.
2. Hypersexuality (Don Juanism in men, and nymphomania in women) is often the result of a sense of sexual inadequacy which the person attempts to disprove and overcome by exaggerated and desperate sexual activity.
3. Daredevil activities (such as being a skydiver, auto racer, or test pilot) are often a response to some deepseated sense of inadequacy or apprehension for which the person attempts to compensate by engaging in flamboyant, spectacular, and fearless activities that few people care to master. Such behavior is sometimes designated as counterphobic.
4. A compulsive dedication to weight-lifting and physical culture often bespeaks an underlying sense of deficiency in some area, and in many instances has originated in response to actual physical inferiority, weakness, or deformity.
5. Persons of limited intelligence sometimes strive to compensate for the deficiency by the affected and inappropriate use of polysyllabic words. Their egregiously sesquipedalian aspirations are preposterous!

Occurrence of Compensation in Normal Behavior

When the normal person finds that he is lacking in some ability that is important to him, he will take special pains to improve himself in that area. The physician who finds a deficiency in one of his therapeutic skills takes postgraduate courses in it, or begins to read a great deal on the topic. Although this is akin to the defense mechanism of compensation, it differs from compensation in several important respects. Such nonpathologic deficits of function are not due to crippling and irrational unconscious conflict or hereditary or acquired deficiency. Since they are conscious, they can be remedied by education. Finally, once the deficit is remedied, it ceases to be a compelling motivation, and does not continue to express itself in behavior.

Efforts to enhance some skill or ability may begin as an attempt to compensate for deficits which are, in fact, rooted in the effects of unconscious conflict. Later, however, such attempts at improvement turn into a more realistic and less defensive activity which has adaptive value for the person and great social value for others. Such efforts then bring realistic satisfactions and become more akin to sublimation than to compensation. The same applies to attitudes and behaviors which originate from the effect of other defenses, especially reaction formation and undoing.

Certain developmentally normal activities demonstrate compensatory behavior. The rowdiness of the preadolescent boy, and the adolescent's fearlessness which often involves recklessness are examples of such activity, although, as noted previously, they may also be rooted in denial (p. 81). Although such compensatory behavior does for a time assist in the defense against conflict over instinctual wishes, especially childlike dependent wishes, they are also developmentally useful attributes which aid in the transition from the normal dependence of childhood to the independence of adulthood. The compensatory efforts to make up for the self doubts which are rampant during adolescence are usually transient, but if such behavior becomes established in an inflexible and repetitious way and is carried into adulthood, it must then be construed as a defense against underlying conflict.

REFERENCES

Bettelheim B: Individual and mass behavior in extreme situations. J Abnorm Soc Psychol 38:417-452, 1943

Erikson EH: Childhood and Society (ed 2). New York, Norton, 1963

Erikson EH: Identity and the life cycle. Psychological Issues, monogr. 1. New York, International Universities, 1959

Freud A: The Ego and the Mechanisms of Defense. New York, International Universities, 1946

Green R: Sexual Identity Conflict in Children and Adults. New York, Basic Books, 1974

Nohain J, Caradec F: Le Petomane. Los Angeles, Sherbourne, 1967

Schafer R: Aspects of Internalization. New York, International Universities, 1968

Stoller R: Sex and Gender. New York, Science, 1968

Stoller R: Facts and fancies: An examination of Freud's concept of bisexuality, in Strouse J (ed): Women and Analysis. New York, Viking, 1974

Sullivan HS: Conceptions of Modern Psychiatry. Washington, William Allanson White Foundation, 1947

4

The Use of Mechanisms of Defense in Normal Behavior

In the earlier sections we described each of the mechanisms of defense and gave examples of their use in the behavior of normal people. Because it is important for the student of behavior to understand that the psychological mechanisms of defense occur in normal as well as abnormal persons, this brief chapter is added to emphasize that point.

All people use defense mechanisms daily. They are used whenever it becomes necessary to prevent an unconscious urge from being expressed overtly in thought or behavior. This occurs whenever internal psychological conflict or the pressure of stressful life events threatens to overwhelm the integration of the Ego, or when Ego functions are weakened by fatigue, illness, brain damage, or toxins such as alcohol. The use of defense mechanisms by normal people is usually transient, and it differs from the frankly pathologic use of defense mechanisms in psychologically disturbed people by being more successfully adaptive and, for the most part, short-lived (a few minutes, hours, or days). In addition, the use of defense mechanisms by normal persons is self-limited, spontaneously recognized, and self-corrected, or, if it does not meet those criteria, it involves only isolated and circumscribed areas of behavior and does not impose major limitations of important functions. In this chapter we shall examine five examples of the use of mechanisms of defense by people who are not clinically or obviously disturbed emotionally. The first three illustrate the transient, spontaneously recognized, and self-correcting use of a defense. The fourth demonstrates a persistent but not pathologic use of reaction formation, and the fifth is an example of a persistent use of undoing that borders on the abnormal.

A CASE OF SELF-LIMITED REGRESSION

The regression experienced by a physician who was hospitalized for a painful and frightening illness can be cited as an example of regression which was self-limited, spontaneously recognized, and corrected. After 2 weeks of treatment which made it necessary for him to be completely bed-ridden, the physician was told by his surgeon that an operation would be performed if no improvement occurred within the next few days. At that point the physician-patient began playfully and only half seriously to read his horoscope in each day's newspaper to see if the fates were for or against him. He learned his surgeon's birthday and jokingly began to follow his doctor's horoscope, too. Surgery became necessary, and on the morning it was to be done, the physician-patient eagerly read both his own and his surgeon's horoscope. To his relief he found that they were both fated by the stars to have a most successful and rewarding day. Although his adult reason told him that the astrological predictions could in no way affect the real outcome of the surgery, he reported that his partial regression to such childlike and magical thinking did protect him to a considerable degree from apprehension and did provide a sense of comfort and reassurance about his future.

A CASE OF SELF-CORRECTING ISOLATION OF AFFECT

A miniobsession which a medical researcher observed in himself may be cited as another example. "Moon Love," a popular song from the 1930s which he had not heard or thought of for 20 years, kept intruding into his awareness. Mentally, he could hear the melody but he could recall only the first line of the words which were, "Is this just moon love, nothing but moon love?" For 2 days the tune harassed him with an obtrusiveness which he likened to the annoyance created by a piece of popcorn wedged between one's teeth. When he finally set about examining his obsession, he realized that it began one morning as soon as he awakened. He then recalled he had worked late the night before on the manuscript of a book, and had felt exhilarated by his fantasy that it would be well received by a colleague who was to give it critical appraisal the next day. At that point in his self-analysis, the rest of the words of the song came back to him: "Is this just moon love, nothing but moon love? Will it be gone when the dawn comes stealing through?" He then realized that he had many misgivings about his brain child, the book, which had seemed so promising the night before. He was haunted by doubt, and feared that in the cold light of dawn the brain child might be considerably less attractive than it had seemed by night. With that realization, the troublesome tune left his head. A few days later, after having received praise from his critic, he awoke with another tune that would not leave his head. The song was "Rock of Ages." Encouraged by the kind words of praise, he now expected his brain child to become a magnificent monument which would endure for all times!

A CASE OF TRANSIENT REPRESSION AND DENIAL

Another colleague reported an additional example of what in 1901 Freud (1960) called the "psychopathology of everyday life." A friend, John, telephoned to tell of his impending marriage to his fiancee, Mora. Consciously, our colleague was delighted at the news, since his friendship with both John and Mora was close and valued. However, a few years earlier he had been greatly saddened when John divorced his first wife, Mary, of whom our colleague was also very fond. In this context, he replied, "John, I am so pleased by this news. Do give my love to Mary!" Immediately, he was painfully aware of his slip in using the first wife's name. After an awkward pause, he tried to rectify matters by saying, "I mean, give my love to Maury!" Again, he realized that he had not used the correct name and that his slip was a combination of Mary and Mora. Only on a third attempt did his tongue do its proper bidding and allow him to say what he had consciously intended in the first place, "I mean, give my love to Mora.'' He had repressed the fiancee's name, Mora. He denied that his friend's first marriage to Mary could not be repaired and eventually resumed. When he attempted to set things right, a compromise was struck between the words Mary and Mora —Maury. Only by conscious effort did he then face reality squarely and say the proper word, Mora. He was torn between his affection for Mary and for Mora, and between his distress at the failure of the first marriage and his joy at the prospect of the second. Repression and denial produced these embarrassing slips of the tongue.

A CASE OF PERSISTENT REACTION FORMATION

Yet another colleague has provided us with an example of a reaction formation in his own behavior. This example also illustrates how irrational and childlike feelings emerge when someone interferes with such a reaction formation. Our colleague is a scholarly person who has great pride in his large library. His books are arranged on shelves in impeccable order. He knows exactly where to find a given volume. This orderly arrangement has great usefulness; he never need lose time searching for a book he wants. His orderliness serves a very realistic and useful function. From time to time his wife or children take a book from the shelf and fail to return it to its proper place. When this occurs, he has noted that he tends to experience childish anger far out of proportion to the minor inconvenience that he has suffered. Thus, his orderliness serves a clearly defensive function: it helps him to maintain control over various circumstances in his life, thus minimizing the chance that he will be frustrated in ways that might trigger his underlying and irrational childish anger.

A CASE OF UNDOING THAT BORDERS ON THE ABNORMAL

Our final example provides an instance of a use of the defense mechanism of undoing which was persistent and was not self-correcting. The person who exhibited it recognized that her behavior was not entirely rational and that it was used to lessen anxiety that had little basis in fact, consequently, this example borders on the pathologic use of a defense mechanism although the defense did not impose any serious limitations on important activities. Because it borders on the pathologic, it is a useful reminder that there is no sharp line between the psychologically normal and abnormal.

A lady of our acquaintance will not go aboard an airplane without first buying flight insurance only at the airport. She insists on purchasing insurance in this manner although she flies a great deal and could buy the same amount of insurance on an annual basis at much less expense. Furthermore, when she journeys to and from a distant city on a roundtrip flight, she ritualistically purchases insurance before each leg of the trip, despite her awareness that the policy purchased before starting the trip also protects her on the return flight.

On one occasion she arrived at the airport too late to purchase insurance and was forced to board the aircraft without performing her ritual. Although she was aware that the flight was the return portion of a roundtrip and she was covered by insurance purchased before leaving her home city, she was exceedingly anxious during the flight and vowed never to fly again without purchasing insurance immediately before boarding the aircraft. Since that time she takes care either to arrive at the airport in time to buy her insurance or when that is not possible, she waits for a later flight in order to make her purchase. By ordinary criteria this woman is psychologically normal, and behaves with reason and intelligence in all spheres of her life except that involved in air travel.

Her remarkable need to purchase insurance in this unusual manner is clearly not dictated by reality. It is obviously a magical gesture designed to ward off a disastrous crash of her airplane. Since we do not know the details of the inner workings of her mental life, we can reasonably assume that this magical act is a symbolic self-immolation. By making a minor sacrifice of money she purchases protection from the fates by atoning through this symbolic sacrifice for some unconscious, deep-seated hostile urge from childhood for which she continues to fear some violent talion punishment. Some long forgotten childish rage is still regarded as being so violent as to deserve violence in return.

REFERENCES

Freud S: The Psychopathology of Everyday Life. Standard Edition, vol 6. London, Hogarth, 1960

5
Mechanisms of Defense
Characteristic of the Major
Clinical Syndromes

In Chapters 2 and 3 we described the various defense mechanisms and cited clinical syndromes to illustrate each. In this chapter we shall reverse this order, and examine the common clinical syndromes and discuss the defense mechanism (or constellation of mechanisms) which is characteristic of each. In doing so, we shall also illustrate another important characteristic of the mechanisms of defense—their tendency to overlap, merge, intertwine, and shade into one another.

For example, although displacement is the mechanism invariably utilized by all people who suffer from phobias, the interplay of impulse and defense, of wish and threat, urge and prohibition is exceedingly complex, and phobic individuals may resort to various other mechanisms in addition to displacement. Consequently, we may see different patterns of defense in different people even though they all have the diagnosis of phobic neurosis. Furthermore, the characteristic pattern of defense used by a given person varies from time to time. This is clearly illustrated by the patient (p. 92) who periodically during her psychoanalytic sessions felt herself to be on the ceiling calmly observing herself enraged on the couch. Diagnostically, her emotional disturbance would be best classified as a depression, a syndrome which primarily involves the use of the mechanism of turning against the self. In the course of therapy she became aware of her intense and infantile rage toward her husband, which in her depressed state she had turned against herself and had not experienced as being directed toward him. When the rage became conscious, it produced intolerable anxiety. At those moments of intolerable anxiety, she resorted to the defense of dissociation. She split her enraged, agitated self from her calm, observing self, and would then report that she felt as if she were situated on the ceiling in a distant corner of the room calmly observing the enraged person who lay on the analytic couch fuming and writhing with hate. Furthermore, we note that this dissociative split into a calm, observing self and a disowned, enraged self involves a regression to that infantile mode of mental functioning through which the small child experiences his good self as quite separate from his bad self. Obviously, not every patient whose condition is diagnosed as a depressive reaction will resort to dissocation as this patient did.

Because of the complexity and fluidity in the interplay of forces in the human being as he attempts to protect himself from conflict, adapt to reality, and secure gratification of his instinctual drives and other needs, diagnoses in the realm of psychopathology lack the precision that they have in other medical specialties. Although diagnostic labels are useful pigeonholes for statistical and other purposes, when human emotions and motivations are concerned, pigeonholes are inadequate. For these reasons the clinical entities that we shall discuss will be considered as *syndromes,* that is, regularly recurring complexes of symptoms and behavioral characteristics which bear sufficient similarity from one patient to the next to warrant having the same diagnostic label.

The invoking of defense mechanisms and the subsequent development of symptoms always has the failure of repression as its starting point. When repression begins to fail, one or more additional mechanisms of defense are called into play. As we have previously indicated, there is often a layering of defenses. For example, as repression begins to fail, conversion may be invoked, and then rationalization added to provide a plausible explanation for the symptoms that conversion produces.

Which defense a given person will resort to is determined by many factors. To illustrate this point let us take a hypothetical example of a pubertal boy who has previously repressed his childhood sexual urges and curiosity. When he is now pressed by the upsurge of sexual drive at adolescence, he may develop, at least transiently, conflict so severe that he must resort to the use of conversion, reaction formation, undoing, or some other additional defense. The question of which additional defense he will now use confronts us with the issue of the choice of defense, a topic to be discussed more fully in Chapter 6. But we must discuss it briefly here.

If our adolescent boy resorts to undoing, say in the form of repetitive prayer or some other religious ritual, he may do so in part out of an identification with his very devout grandfather. If his undoing takes the form of unnecessary bathing several times daily, it may be the result of an identification with his father who is scrupulous about personal cleanliness. In addition to identification with particular family members, the prevailing style and atmosphere of family life is often a factor in determining which specific mechanism of defense a person will use. Furthermore, we would assume in the instance of this particular young man that undue emphasis on cleanliness and control had occurred during his early childhood, resulting in a fixation at the mode of magical thought which characterizes the 3-year-old. The tendency to resort to magical thought which such a fixation produces will predispose the person to the use of undoing in adolescence and adulthood.

Another adolescent reared in a family atmosphere that unduly emphasizes the need for caution in meeting potentially dangerous situations in life may resort to the use of displacement and develop a phobia, for example an irrational fear of dancing, dating, or other situations that stir his feared sexual urges.

The study of the various clinical syndromes will help clarify the layering of defenses. Characteristically when one defense threatens to fail, another mechanism is brought into play to bolster the defensive operations. When some of the mechanisms fail, they tend regularly to be bolstered by other predictably specific defenses. For example, when we see the defense of projection in operation, it is safe to assume that there has been an antecedent but inadequate use of denial. Thus, when the small child blames his tricycle for crashing into the coffee table, we can readily infer the antecedent denial, "I did not do it." This denial is then followed by the accusatory projection, "It was the tricycle that did it."

In a similar fashion, when we see a reaction formation in operation, it is probable that there has been some preceding identification. For instance, when a small child has suffered several scoldings at the hands of his mother for pinching the new baby, he tends progressively to identify with the mother's prohibitions about pinching the baby and at the same time to identify with his mother's attitude of concern and solicitude for the infant. By means of identification he develops kindly attitudes toward the baby, attitudes exactly opposite to his underlying hateful wishes to pinch and hurt. Thus a reaction formation is born, which now helps him to control primitive hostility toward his rival.

The specific behavior that a given person may exhibit often does not allow us to determine easily whether that behavior is, in fact, a defense or, if it is, which defense it may represent. For example, when a person responds with lack of concern or grief to the death of a very important person he may be resorting to denial, or he may be resorting to some form of identification with the lost person if the dead person was very stoic and undemonstrative. Only if we get more details about his background are we able to decide whether he has resorted to the defense of identification or denial. Denial refutes the reality of the loss, and the person does not acknowledge that it has actually occurred. On the other hand, if the person has resorted to identification as a defense against the loss, he acknowledges the reality of the loss, but he adopts the stoicism and unemotional attitude that characterized the dead person. By this identification he retains his relationship with the deceased, and the anguish of the loss is partially attenuated. These two examples demonstrate that the behavior of emotional unresponsiveness to a death can represent either the use of denial or the defense of identification, and that there is no one-to-one relationship between a given type of behavior and the use of a given mechanism of defense. Only when we know the inner experience and psychological reality of the person concerned can we determine whether a particular behavior represents the use of a mechanism of defense, or even which defense it is.

Although broad patterns of defensive operations tend to characterize a given person and to be used in a given clinical syndrome, the detailed ingredients which determine which person will use what defense are very complex, and the factors involved are forever changing, intermixing, ebbing, and flowing. However, we wish again to emphasize the basic principles which are involved in the development of all clinical syndromes. First, anxiety and the mechanisms of defense which it triggers are responsible for the formation of symptoms. Second, the fundamental or primary mechanism of defense is repression, and it is only when repression begins to fail that other mechanisms are called into play and symptoms form. When repression is successful, there is no anxiety and there are no overt symptoms to be observed.

ANXIETY NEUROSES

Description

All people experience anxiety, a diffuse feeling state characterized by apprehension, dread, and the activation of the autonomic nervous system. Anxiety is always unpleasant—in its most extreme form, panic, it severely disrupts normal psychological functioning. When anxiety is the principal symptom and persists or recurs regularly, the diagnosis of an anxiety neurosis can be made. The person with an anxiety neurosis is unaware of the source of his anxiety. He suffers from a pervasive sense of impending but nameless disaster. The stormy hyperactivity of his autonomic nervous system often produces frightening somatic symptoms, such as tachycardia, palpitation, sweating, dizziness, dry mouth, difficult swallowing, digestive disturbances, urinary frequency, impotence, hyperventilation, or various other unpleasant disturbances. The person who suffers from this condition often fears either impending death or impending insanity, or both.

In 1895, Freud first gave this syndrome the label of *anxiety neurosis.* Initially, he considered the disturbance to be the result of inadequate release of sexual drive resulting in a damming up of sexual tension, with the concomitant damming up of sexual substances and the creation of a biochemical toxic state. Currently, we consider anxiety neurosis to be the consequence of a chronic threat that instinctual drives may overwhelm the Ego and exceed its capacity to master, control, and find acceptable modes of expression for those drives.

Defense Mechanisms Characteristic of Anxiety Neuroses

Anxiety neurosis occurs when there is a chronic but partial and relative failure of the basic defense mechanism, repression. When repression, for whatever reason or combination of reasons, proves to be inadequate, previously contained primitive instinctual urges threaten to come to expression, and this threat creates the sense of apprehension characteristic of this neurosis. The result is a kind of cold war between unconscious instinctual drives and the controls of the Ego, and a chronic state of mobilization obtains with episodes of greater alarm from time to time. When the controlling, organizing, and defensive functions of the Ego remain sufficiently mobilized, no further mechanisms of defense are called up to join the battle. However, the chronic mobilization creates chronic tension and anxiety. If the anxiety becomes overwhelming, either chronically or episodically, other defenses are then mobilized, and the anxiety neurosis changes into another syndrome—a phobia, for example, or a dissociative state (as in the instance of the patient who periodically found herself watching from the ceiling of the analytic office while the "other person" on the couch was filled with rage). A phobia develops when the patient objectifies his apprehension and no longer experiences a pervasive, nameless sense of impending disaster. The apprehension now becomes attached to a specific object or situation. If he can then avoid that situation, he is relatively free of anxiety.

PHOBIC NEUROSES

Description

A *phobia* is an irrational fear of some person, object, or situation. When the person suffering from a phobia is exposed to the situation he fears, he experiences intense anxiety. If he is forced into intimate or prolonged exposure to the phobic situation, panic may occur and his Ego functions may disorganize severely, resulting in the inability to function effectively.

The phobic person may recognize that his symptomatic fear is unduly exaggerated or inappropriate. He is frequently at a loss to explain his fear, and may resort to clever rationalizations to give his symptom the gloss of logic—as in the instance of a man with a phobia of elevators who explained his invariable use of the stairway as an evidence of his dedication to maintaining physical fitness through exercise.

Many people experience some degree of irrational apprehension in certain circumstances such as being in high places, near certain animals, or aboard an aircraft. Such irrational fears are usually not considered evidence of a neurosis when they are mild or limited to unimportant matters. However, if such fears impose significant limitations on important activities, and the person's life becomes organized around his need to avoid the phobic situation, the diagnosis of neurosis is warranted. In many instances, phobias tend to spread and involve more and more areas of a person's life. A mild but irrational fear of germs may eventually lead to a tormented life submerged in disinfectants, or a phobia of open spaces may ultimately confine a person to his home.

Defense Mechanisms
Characteristic of Phobic Neuroses

When repression is weakened as a result of any combination of factors and hitherto excluded unacceptable impulses threaten to emerge in awareness, the person is warned of this threat by the appearance of anxiety. Often, a person who later develops a phobia has an initial transient period of anxiety that is unrelated to any apparent cause or situation. He then connects his apprehension to some suitable symbolic object or situation, and experiences his apprehension as being caused by that object or situation. Through this mechanism of displacement, a phobia replaces the original free-floating anxiety. In other instances, there is no transient period of free-floating anxiety; the phobia seems to arise *de novo*. In either case, the person then copes with his anxiety by avoiding the phobic situation. If forced into the phobic situation, anxiety or even panic results, and other mechanisms may be called forth—a conversion reaction causing blindness, a dissociation with amnesia, or a further regression with the psychotic use of projection in the form of hallucinations and delusions, are but a few. Some degree of regression is, of course, inherent in phobic reactions since the development of a phobia involves a return to the primitive modes of thought through which the small child copes with his own threatening impulses. In Chapter 6, we shall describe how a patient with a phobia of thunderstorms resorted to an even more extreme regression and became psychotic when unduly vigorous therapeutic efforts forced on her a sudden realization of the murderous rage against which her phobia defended.

HYSTERICAL NEUROSES

Description

A hysterical neurosis produces symptoms of two types: (1) disturbances of motor or sensory functions which result in physical symptoms such as paralyses, anesthesias, or pain (this type of hysterical neurosis is designated as hysterical neurosis, conversion type); and (2) disturbances of purely mental functions which produce symptoms such as amnesia, fugue states, or instances of multiple personality (this type of disorder is designated as hysterical neurosis, dissociative type). The person with hysterical symptoms classically exhibits a remarkable indifference and lack of concern about his symptoms, even dramatically disabling symptoms such as paralysis of all extremities or pain about which he constantly complains. Usually the symptoms of hysterical disturbance involve motor, sensory, or mental functions that are normally under voluntary control. However, sometimes hysterical symptoms involve functions that are controlled by the autonomic nervous system, for example, psychogenic impotence.

When the hysterical patient is pressed to explain the cause of his symptoms, he often resorts to elaborate rationalizations. This is exemplified by the person with hysterical paralysis who blames his problem on some prior injury insisting that it caused his paralysis. Rationalization of this type is often used when a law suit or insurance settlement is pending. When a hysterical neurosis results from conflict over hostile impulses, the defense mechanism of turning against the self is commonly involved, so that the patient's own body becomes the target of his own hostile aggression. Hysterical vomiting during pregnancy is an example. In this condition the pregnant woman harbors hostile feelings toward the fetus which she has psychologically rejected, and her vomiting is a symbolic representation of this rejection. Her wish to get rid of that which is inside of her produces the vomiting, which in turn inflicts discomfort on her, and in extreme instances leads to serious consequences such as dehydration and malnutrition.

Defense Mechanisms Characteristic of Hysterical Neuroses

Hysterical symptoms, like all symptoms, occur when repression, the basic mechanism of defense, fails. In hysterical conditions characterized by physical symptoms, conversion is the mechanism next called into play, and is the defense mechanism utilized in hysterical neuroses, conversion type. It is usually bolstered by other mechanisms of defense as previously noted. When the symptoms of a hysterical neurosis involve purely psychological functions, the defense mechanism of dissociation is the one called on when repression fails and is the defense mechanism characteristic of hysterical neuroses, dissociative type. In this condition, as repression fails and unconscious disowned impulses threaten to emerge into awareness, anxiety evokes the mechanism of dissociation. Through this mechanism, disowned functions and impulses are split off or dissociated from the normal waking aspect of the personality. These disowned impulses gain ascendancy and emerge as behavior which is excluded from awareness when the person is in his usual state of mental functioning. Consequently he is amnesic for the behavior that took place during the period of dissociation. Like the person with conversion symptoms, the person with symptoms caused by dissociation characteristically appears unconcerned about his symptomatic behavior. For example, despite a dramatic inability to remember what occurred during a period of amnesia, such a person is remarkably unperturbed by his loss of memory.

When the disowned aspects of personality which emerge during dissociation are sufficiently organized and complete so as to have a distinct identity, a case of multiple personality develops. Generally, dissociation does not produce the dramatic syndrome of multiple personality. Rather, it takes the form of a disturbance of consciousness which may range from episodes of vague and uncertain memory to periods of total amnesia or even stupor. Occasionally, in states of altered consciousness the person is "taken over," and, in a sense, possessed by unconscious forces and motivations which cause him to perform highly organized and complex activities. In such periods, he may appear normal to the outside observer. The patient has no recollection later of the activities performed during his fugue state.

Identification is almost invariably involved in the production of symptoms which result either from the use of the mechanism of conversion or the mechanism of dissociation. Whether the hysterical person suffers from physical symptoms such as paralysis or mental symptoms such as amnesia, a detailed history usually reveals that some significant person in the patient's life has manifested an identical or very similar condition. Identification with this significant person plays an important role in the symptom formation.

Hysterical neuroses also involve regression insofar as they produce a return to a childlike state of helplessness and dependence on others. Even more profound regression may result if the defenses of dissociation or conversion are too vigorously attacked in the course of psychotherapy. For example, we can cite the instance of a young man who developed total amnesia for all of the events which surrounded a hunting accident in which he killed his older brother. When the psychiatrist used a sodium amytal interview in an ill advised and hasty effort to have the patient retrieve the memory of these events, they burst again into the patient's conscious awareness, overwhelming the capacity of his Ego to handle them. He was flooded with anxiety and guilt, and immediately disorganized into a profoundly psychotic state which included the understandable delusion that the doctor was persecuting him.

OBSESSIVE–COMPULSIVE NEUROSES

Description

The obsessive–compulsive neurosis is characterized by obsessive thoughts and compulsive acts. An *obsessive thought* repeatedly intrudes into awareness and cannot be stopped from doing so. Although obsessive thoughts occur in a limitless variety of forms such as a fantasy, song, wish, word, sentence, or prayer, they commonly fall into one of two general categories. (1) They may be of a personally offensive or frightening nature, such as blasphemous thoughts, recurring preoccupations with perverse sexual actions, or thoughts of committing some murderous act, or (2) they may be of an inconsequential, trivial, and silly type, such as nonsense phrases, neologisms, fragments of poetry, counting, or outlandish ruminations about philosophical or theological issues. For example, a young intellectual patient was harassed by the recurrent question, "Were the Waldenses in fact correct?". This was a reflection of his conflict over the control of his own base impulses. The connection between the obsessive thought and the impulses to which it symbolically refers, becomes clear if one knows the basic tenet of the Waldenses. The Waldenses were a sect of dissenters from Catholicism founded in 1170 by Peter Waldo who sought to revive pureness of living among his followers.

Many normal people occasionally experience transient obsessional phenomena, an example of which is a tune that recurs in their thoughts in an uncontrollable and annoying manner. Another frequently encountered obsession is the so-called doubting mania which leads the person to repetitive acts designed to reassure him that he either has or has not done a certain thing. A normal version of such doubting is the occasional experience of uncertainty as to whether one has locked a door, turned off a stove, and the like. When an obsessional thought becomes clearly pathologic, it is always unpleasant, persistent, and beyond the person's ability to control, no matter how hard he tries.

Compulsions are repetitious, ritualistic acts which a person feels compelled to carry out. The person concerned may feel that his compulsive acts are absurd and senseless, but he is powerless to prevent them. If anything interferes or prevents him from enacting his compulsive rituals, he invariably becomes anxious and sometimes panicky. This betrays the defensive nature of the compulsion and the manner in which it helps to prevent anxiety. Compulsive rituals may assume any form, but certain acts are common such as compulsive and repetitive handwashing, stylized avoidance techniques (such as taking care not to step on lines on a sidewalk or to walk under ladders), irresistible urges to count objects (sometimes further complicated by the need to divide and subdivide the totals into even or odd figures), and ceremonials around the act of touching (for example, a well-known and very seclusive public figure is said to be so concerned about germs that he never shakes hands or touches a door knob without first donning gloves).

Defense Mechanisms Characteristic of Obsessive–Compulsive Neuroses

Three defense mechanisms are characteristic of the obsessive–compulsive neuroses: isolation of affect, undoing, and reaction formation. In this condition, when repression begins to fail, one or more of these three mechanisms come into play. *Isolation of affect* is responsible for the symptom of obsessional thoughts, *undoing* creates compulsive acts, and *reaction formation* accounts for scrupulosity and other exaggerated characteristics of kindness, cleanliness, solicitude, and generosity.

The formation of an obsessional thought occurs by the following process. As repression fails, an unconscious primitive impulse forces its way into awareness as a thought. Through the mechanisms of isolation of affect, the thought is split off from the affect that would normally coincide with it. The affect is excluded from awareness and the thought, devoid of its appropriate affect, is experienced as neutral or indifferent or foreign or absurd; the person who experiences such a thought feels that it does not truly belong to him because it does not express anything that he wants or feels. For example, the young mother who has the recurrent obsessional thought, "Kill the baby" can truthfully say that she has no feelings of anger towards her child, despite the clear presence of hostility which her thought betrays. As abhorrent as such a thought is, it is not as abhorrent and disturbing as it would be if it were accompanied by feelings of murderous anger.

The symptom of a compulsive act is sometimes formed in two steps: (1) a disowned impulse either threatens to emerge or actually does emerge in overt expression either as a thought or as a disguised symbolic gesture, and (2) this expression of the forbidden urge is then followed by another act which symbolically and magically undoes, cancels, or counteracts it. In other instances the initial forbidden urge remains unconscious and only the second defensive act, the magical ritual of undoing, is consciously experienced. In either instance, the compulsive act which the person feels driven to perform represents a ritual which magically undoes or counteracts a forbidden unconscious impulse as exemplified in the handwashing compulsion which symbolically counteracts some "dirty" urge.

The obsessive–compulsive person also defends against his urges by the use of reaction formation—the development of attitudes and behaviors which are exactly opposite to the impulses being defended against. Undoing, isolation of affect, and especially reaction formation often stem, in part, from the process of identification with people significant in the person's formative childhood years. These are the people who disciplined him and who opposed the expression of his primitive impulses. They frequently were people who themselves exhibited compulsive personality traits, and thus provided a model for the use of isolation, undoing, and reaction formation.

The use of other mechanisms can also be observed in many obsessive-compulsive patients. Displacement is often apparent in the formation of pathological fears which then leads to the development of compulsive rituals, as exemplified by the person with a dread of germs who subsequently develops a handwashing compulsion. Rationalization is often used to give plausible and logical reasons for irrational compulsive rituals. Turning against the self may also occur, and is exemplified by the compulsive handwasher who scrubs his hands until they are raw and bleeding. Of course, regression is essential for the development of an obsessive–compulsive neurosis. The magical power of the obsessional thought and compulsive act is a reflection of regression to the modes of thought characteristic of the child at the age of 2 to 3 years.

DEPRESSIVE REACTIONS

Description

Depression is one of the most common psychiatric symptoms. Almost all people experience this disagreeable affective state, at least transiently and episodically. Originating from a childhood response to loss of parental love, the affect of depression in later life may be evoked by a variety of losses, real or symbolic. Bereavement is a naturally occurring experiment that dramatically exemplifies the relationship of loss and depression. This relationship has been elucidated by Parkes (1972). The types of losses which are clinically important include:

1. Loss of a relationship with an emotionally important person (among the causes of such a loss are death, divorce, the waning of affection, and geographical separation)
2. Loss of health, important body functions, physical attractiveness, or physical or mental capacities due to disease, injury, or aging
3. Loss of status or prestige (that is, loss of esteem in the eyes of others)
4. Loss of self-esteem
5. Loss of occupational or financial security
6. Loss of a fantasy, or, more precisely, the loss of hope of fulfillment of an important fantasy
7. Loss of a symbol, usually referred to as a symbolic loss

The first five of these categories of loss are easily understood and involve losses that are obvious and real. Category 6, loss of hope of fulfillment of an important fantasy, usually accompanies a real loss, and may be more devastating than the real loss itself. The case of a ski instructor who sustained a fracture of his leg which was so severe that it would prevent him from ever jumping again in competition, illustrates a devastating symbolic loss which accompanies a moderate real loss. Although his fracture would not prevent him from working in the future as a ski instructor, it did put an end to any hope of his realizing the fantasy of winning a gold medal as a ski jumper in the Olympics, a secret fantasy which had been an important sustaining factor in the young man's psychological integration for some years. Although his injury was not extremely serious by ordinary standards, and by those standards did not impose serious loss, it did produce a severe depressive reaction because it involved the loss of hope of ever attaining an important fantasy. Another example of this type of loss of a fantasy is a person who overidealizes a friend, lover, or mate, and then becomes depressed when the other person proves incapable of living up to the fantasied expectations.

Category 7, the loss of a symbol (usually referred to as a symbolic loss), is exemplified by the case of a sports car enthusiast. This man, age 49, had for years been an avid competitor in sports car rallies in his area. For several years he had regularly won most events, a feat he largely attributed to the outstanding performance of his sleek, immaculately cared-for crimson Ferrari. Despite the fact that the automobile was fully covered by insurance and could be replaced, he became significantly depressed when it burned up. To this man there could never be another Ferrari such as the one he had lost. Obviously his sports car was an important symbol of something he valued highly and was desperately afraid of losing. Psychoanalytic treatment revealed that this man's Ferrari symbolically represented several things which he felt he was in the process of losing—youth, agility, physical attractiveness, and sexual potency, to name a few.

In summary, losses which evoke depression may be real, symbolic, or the loss of an important fantasy. Most commonly, losses which are sufficiently painful to produce a significant degree of depression involve all or some combination of three types of loss. The case of the bereaved mother cited in a subsequent part of this chapter demonstrates how a real loss by death of a son also involved both the loss of a fantasy and of a symbol.

When a persistent mood of morbid depression is the principal symptom of a psychiatric illness, the diagnosis of depressive reaction is warranted. In this section on depressive reactions we shall ignore the controversial question of whether there is any fundamental difference, except of degree, between a neurotic depressive reaction and a psychotic depressive reaction. We shall also ignore the controversy over whether some depressions are reactive (a response to some distressing life event) and others endogenous (due to some biochemical disturbance, perhaps genetically determined, rather than being a response to a distressing life event). For a fuller discussion of these and other unsettled issues regarding the cause and treatment of depressive illnesses, see the excellent monograph by Beck (1967) and the volume of papers edited by Scott and Senay (1973).

In our own experience, when depressive reactions are carefully studied they are always found to involve a response to loss, although we readily grant that some biologic factor, perhaps genetic in origin, predisposes some people to become depressed in response to losses which other persons might bear with little or no difficulty. Traumatic events in childhood, especially loss of or separation from parents, constitute another group of factors which predispose a person to respond with depression to traumatic events in later life, as Heinicke (1973), Beck (1967), and others have suggested. Whatever may be the interplay of genetic, biochemical, and experiential factors in the production of depression, those cases of depression which occur in response to a demonstrable loss involve similar psychodynamics whether the depressed state takes the form of a suicidal psychosis or a period of low mood in a relatively normal person.

When one is depressed, he lacks in some degree the ability to take interest in or derive pleasure from any activity, and he feels empty and desolate. Life seems futile, the future appears bleak, and the desire to carry on is sapped. There is loss of pleasure in sex, food, friends, family, work, or hobbies. Refreshing sleep is not possible, energy is low, and even ordinary responsibilities seem like insuperable tasks.

In more severe forms of depression the sense of hopelessness and futility becomes total. The patient is unable to eat and loses weight, he is unable to sleep the whole night, he is impotent or incapable of being sexually aroused, and he has various somatic symptoms such as indigestion, headache, chest pain, constipation, and fatigue. In depressions of psychotic proportions delusions of guilt and worthlessness appear, and somatic delusions that body organs have rotted or other bizarre ideas of decay or loss occur. The depressed person may hear voices which accuse him of various foul deeds and unspeakable sins. When feelings of hopelessness, worthlessness, or guilt become unbearable, suicide is common. Characteristically, depressive disorders tend to occur in very compulsive people who are conscientious to a fault. Never having been able to live up to the dictates of an excessively harsh and vindictive Superego, the depressed person falls victim to the unrealistic criticisms and insatiable demands of his own conscience.

Such a conscience (and the ambivalence that is inherent in the obsessive–compulsive person with such a conscience) is the seedbed from which pathologic depression springs. The person who is always under criticism from a relentlessly harsh conscience tends to be overly dependent on love, goodwill, and praise from others to counteract his constant inner sense of worthlessness. Consequently, he is especially vulnerable to loss of love and the loss of relationships with people from whom he seeks to obtain reassurance of his worth. This childlike dependence on others for emotional support makes for relationships which are inherently ambivalent; that is, because the person feels tyrannized by those on whose approval his self-esteem so desperately depends, he is prone to hate the very people he loves and needs. Whenever his expectations and need for love are not fulfilled, underlying rage erupts. His harsh conscience and perfectionistic obsessive–compulsive defenses make his own hostility difficult for him to accept or even acknowledge, and he frequently turns it back on himself.

The relationship of morbid depression to loss, ambivalence, and the way in which loss unleashes the hostile component of an ambivalent relationship is exemplified in the case of a patient whose son unexpectedly died. The mother of a handsome, bright, and very promising teenage boy was devastated by his death from acute leukemia which became manifest only 2 weeks earlier. At first she refused to believe that the diagnosis was correct. When the chemotherapy of the leukemia was ineffective, she became enraged at the very competent physician who was treating her son. Being a deeply religious person, she began to pray when the son's death was obviously imminent, bargaining with God by promising to do various acts of religious devotion and sacrifice if He would only spare her son. When her son died, she flew into a rage, first at the doctor, then at God whom she loved and revered, and finally at the son she adored. She grabbed a knife and made wild threats to kill the physician, she cursed God and vowed never to go to church again, and finally she screamed and pounded on the body of her son, wailing "Don't do this to me—you're not being fair. Come back, come back."

This unfortunate woman suffered a variety of losses. She sustained a real loss in the death of this very attractive son whose bright future was an important sustaining factor in her life. She also sustained a severe symbolic loss in that her son was an important symbol of her sense of worth and accomplishment, especially so because she had two other children with serious congenital defects. Finally, the boy's death caused the loss of a very important fantasy —that she who was so devout would be protected by some magical and omnipotent outside agent. This fantasy was smashed when first the doctor failed to bring about a miraculous cure, and next God whom she had worshiped faithfully, failed to spare her son from death. This combination of real loss, symbolic loss, and loss of a fantasy left her temporarily disorganized, frightened, hurt, and angry, much as a small child feels when deserted by his parents. Next, she refused to eat or move from bed because, she stated, since her son could no longer move or eat, neither could she. Finally, she became depressed, threatened suicide, and berated herself for not having fed her son properly and not having made him obtain more rest, failings on her part which she insisted were responsible for his leukemia.

In these observations of a naturally occurring experiment on the effect of loss, we can see the causes and the defenses involved in a case of depression of extreme degree. The mother's relationship with her son was ambivalent, as is apparent in the personal gain which she demanded from the promise of her son's future. He was unduly regarded as a supplier of esteem and support, and her love for him was tinged with these selfish needs. His impending loss badly disrupted her Ego-organizing and Ego-controlling functions. She regressed, looking in a childlike fashion to the doctor to perform a godlike miracle. When he could not do this, her rage at him erupted. Then she turned to God. When He performed no miracle in response to her prayers, she became enraged at Him. When all hope was lost, she turned her anger on her dead son. Her anger subsided when she resorted to identification with the lost person, becoming unable to eat or move from her bed. Finally, she turned her anger on herself in the depressive self-accusatory idea that she was somehow responsible for causing her son's fatal illness. Her self-accusations were intoned in a manner very reminiscent of her earlier complaints at her son for deserting her. Here, we can see that her identification with the dead boy allowed her symbolically to maintain the relationship with him, and that some of her self-accusations were accusations directed toward him, now within herself.

Mechanisms of Defense Characteristic of Depressive Reactions

Loss results in depression. The affect of depression signals that a loss has occurred or is anticipated. When depression does not reach a clearly morbid degree, the affect and its physiological concomitants probably represent nothing more than the biologically innate response to loss. In less severe but nonetheless pathologic forms of depression, that is depression out of proportion to the reality of the loss, the loss produces regression and revives the intense sense of hopelessness and despair that the small child experiences when the parents are absent for an extended time. In the most extreme types of depression in which morbid guilt, self-accusations of worthlessness, and extreme hopelessness occur, we can see the effect of identification with the lost object and the use of the mechanism of turning aggression against the self. The hostile component of the ambivalent relationship to the lost person is primitive and destructive. In turning such infantile aggression against the self, much of the hostility intended for the lost person is turned against the lost person who now, through the process of identification, is symbolically within the depressed person. When the rage which is turned against the self becomes extreme, suicide results as a symbolic murder of the lost person with whom the suicide victim has identified.

MANIC STATES

Description

The manic person is superficially the opposite of the depressed person. Elated, euphoric, hyperactive, and expansive, he races about with seemingly boundless energy, enthusiasm, and optimism. He talks incessantly, sleeps little, and is forever in action. He is omnipotent, regal, and arrogant in his attitudes. He frantically evolves schemes for making untold amounts of money, solving the problems of the world, and setting social wrongs right. Although he often regards himself as a Messiah or genius, he spends money foolishly, involves himself in love affairs or business ventures frantically, and in general shows an impaired ability to grasp reality correctly or to foresee consequences realistically. Anyone who interferes with his mad rush of ideas and activities is angrily attacked. He becomes paranoid at times, accusing those who interfere or question him of being too stupid to understand his brilliance and the importance of his schemes, or of being so envious that they intend to harm him. He is, above all else, *correct*, and all who differ are fools or persecutors.

However, this facade of optimism is very thin. It is a defensive response to the same sense of loss to which the depressed person has reacted with despair. When one talks with a manic patient at length, the patient from time to time will invariably touch on some topic that causes him momentary depression. His voice quivers and tears come to his eyes. He then immediately rebounds to his state of forced and pressured optimism, cheerfulness, and megalomanic omnipotence. In short, his optimism and energetic hyperactivity is a coverup for an underlying sense of depression. The depression that lurks beneath the manic mood is readily discernible in the responses that manic patients give to projective psychological tests such as the Rorschach. Frequently, the manic mood is terminated by the onset of depression, or a period of depression is terminated by the onset of mania.

Questions similar to those noted in the section on depressive reactions can be raised regarding the genetic and biochemical factors in manic states. We will again limit our discussion to the psychological reaction observable in the manic patient, and refer our reader to Goodwin and Bunney (1973) for a resume of the more purely biological aspects of depression and mania.

Defense Mechanisms Characteristic of Manic States

Denial is the defense mechanism characteristic of mania. Like depression, mania is the reaction to a loss. When the loss is defended against by denial, the affect of depression does not occur. Since the loss is denied, there is no need to feel sad; indeed, the triumphant refutation of the loss calls forth the opposite effect, elation. But reality continuously assaults the irrational denial, and the patient must strive ever more frantically to maintain his denial by not only refusing to acknowledge his loss but also by maintaining a reactive sense of triumph, power, optimism, and omnipotence—a state of mind opposite to the sense of helplessness and hopelessness that usually occurs in response to loss. To maintain this unrealistic sense of omnipotence and elation, an ever-increasing use of denial is necessary to refute those aspects of reality which challenge the patient's omnipotence and grandiosity. When denial is threatened, the manic patient may then resort to projection, attributing his own anger to others in the belief that it is their malicious intent or stupidity which causes them to question his expansive schemes. Regression is also prominent in the manic state, which clearly involves a return to the magical thinking characteristic of the very small child. Whatever genetic or biochemical factors may be involved in the etiology of mania and depression, the psychological factors are obvious and are responsible for the specific symptoms in a given case.

PARANOID CONDITIONS

Description

The irrational attribution to others of one's disowned primitive urges, especially hostile urges, is a central feature of the paranoid mode, and the use of the defense mechanism of projection is the central psychodynamic factor in paranoid states. The tendency to externalize blame and to disown unworthy needs and motivations is a universal human characteristic. The use of paranoid mechanisms by psychologically normal people is exemplified in the instance (cited in the section on projection, p. 84) of the physician who cursed and in effect accused the inert and immobile concrete curb of attacking his tires when, out of his own carelessness, he ran into the curb while parking his car. At the other end of the spectrum lies the paranoid schizophrenic who rambles on in a confused, disorganized discourse as he describes bizarre delusional beliefs that someone or something is persecuting him. Between these extremes, we find the person whose entire character structure is built around a basic mistrust of other people. He is not psychotic or even greatly impaired in his ability to cope with life, but he is prickly and defensive in his dealings with people, and arrogant in the insistence that his views and beliefs are *the* correct ones. Everyone else is, at best, wrong or stupid, or even may be deliberately attempting to betray or defeat him. Further toward the grossly psychotic end of the spectrum we encounter the condition diagnosed as *paranoid state*. This disorder is represented by the person who harbors subtle and cleverly rationalized persecutory and paranoid delusions, but who is sufficiently intact psychologically in other respects that the irrational nature of his paranoid beliefs is difficult to detect. Such a person often becomes the messianic leader of extremist groups, as, for example, the political far right and far left. Which side of the political system he embraces is immaterial as long as there is an opposing group who can be viewed as the enemy who must be defeated by any means, including violence.

Defense Mechanisms Characteristic of Paranoid Conditions

Reliance on the defense mechanism of projection characterizes paranoid disorders. The use of this mechanism as the predominant defense is the basis of paranoid symptoms, whether they be harmless and transient externalizations as used by the above-cited car driver or the bizarre and obviously psychotic delusions of the paranoid schizophrenic. In all instances of paranoid symptoms, disowned and threatening impulses (usually hostile) which the person himself harbors are externalized and attributed to others. This results in the ability to say, "It is not I who has hostile and destructive urges toward other people, on the contrary, it is they who hate and attempt to hurt me—me, who is blameless and innocent. But since they persecute me, I am justified in hating them."

Regression is inherent in the production of paranoid delusions, since such delusions are possible only in one who thinks in primitive modes characterized by the inability to distinguish realistically between a troubling and frightening impulse within himself and a threatening intent on the part of someone or something outside of himself. For the paranoid person, rationalization is a valued and constant companion to projection. The paranoid person's ability to give plausible and logical reasons for his irrational paranoid beliefs is monumental. In this way he conceals his irrationality from himself and from the world.

THE SCHIZOPHRENIAS

Description

The group of more or less similar psychiatric disorders labeled *schizophrenia* constitute the area of greatest scientific controversy and uncertainty in the field of psychiatry. Some cases of schizophrenia seem to result from overwhelming environmental stress, such as may be encountered from prolonged exposure to combat in wartime. For example, some soldiers who became psychotic in combat in World War II showed all of the signs and symptoms of schizophrenia, yet a few days or weeks later, when they were examined in a military hospital in the United States, they showed no evidence of schizophrenia or of any significant emotional disorder. With rest and removal from the stress of combat, these soldiers reintegrated spontaneously. Other cases seem to be largely the product of traumatic childhood experiences and disturbed patterns of communication and relationships within the family. Lidz (1973) has admirably summarized this point of view.

Other authorities consider the cause of schizophrenia to be some biochemical disorder, probably genetically determined. This point of view has been most ably summarized by Kety (1972) and his associates (Wender et al, 1974).

No matter what weight one chooses to give genetic endowment, possible biochemical disorder, traumatic childhood experience, family pathology, or environmental stress in the etiology of schizophrenia, the primitive, chaotic, and irrational mode of thought as well as the delusions and hallucinations which characterize schizophrenia are understandable from the psychoanalytic point of view and demonstrate the use of various mechanisms of defense, most notably projection and regression.

In 1911, Bleuler, who coined the term *schizophrenia*, gave us the first systematic study of the psychopathologic processes involved in this group of disorders. His basic notions have not been greatly improved on since. He observed that the schizophrenic disorder is characterized by a specific and illogic mode of associating one idea with another. This disturbance in the association of thoughts renders the speech of the schizophrenic patient chaotic and difficult to understand. Bleuler also noted the disturbance in affect which causes the schizophrenic person to exhibit emotions which are inappropriate to the ideas he expresses. For example, a schizophrenic patient giggled and laughed as he told of his delusions that his lungs had rotted and that he continuously smelled the stench of their decay. A third characteristic of schizophrenia described by Bleuler is autism. This refers to the schizophrenic person's tendency to live and feel and think in a very private and idiosyncratic manner, being more responsive to his inner urges and experiences than to the demands of external reality. The fourth and final characteristic of schizophrenia that Bleuler described is ambivalence. This refers to the presence of a paralyzing and offsetting mixture of love and hate in relationships with people.

Another notable defect in the mental functions of the schizophrenic person is his lack of adequate Ego boundaries, that is, lack of a clear sense of self and non-self. He is easily confused about which feelings, urges, or emotions belong to him, and which reside in or emanate from other people. This phenomenon is, of course, only one manifestation of the most global defect seen in the schizophrenic person—defective reality testing. *Defective reality testing* refers to the inability to determine the difference between what is objectively real and what is subjectively experienced in a private and idiosyncratic fashion.

The term *schizophrenia* literally means *splitting of the mind.* The splitting in this instance does not refer to the kind of splitting of personality which we discussed in the section on the mechanism of dissociation (p. 90) and which occurs in cases of multiple personality. Rather, it refers to the fragmentation of mental processes and the discordance of thought, feeling, and behavior which is so prominent in the schizophrenias.

The clinical picture of schizophrenia in its most extreme form is often the basis for the stereotype of the insane person. Bizarre thoughts, wild delusional ideas, and weird hallucinations are seen in severe cases. But often the only discernible evidence of psychosis is the patient's peculiar mode of thought. Most psychiatrists would agree that the presence of this characteristic thought disorder is the one essential feature that is necessary to make the diagnosis. Schizophrenic thought is hard to describe, especially in its subtle forms. We will, therefore, resort to a rather florid example to illustrate the nature of schizophrenic thought.

A physician asked a severely schizophrenic patient, "What problems made it necessary for you to come to the hospital?", to which the patient replied, "It was heath-kit and sigma-seven. A dune buggy sun landing strip. Science! Satellites and a karate chop, like heath-kit. Boxing on an airplane hangar. Tarzan! Father! Aba! Father! Judas! Thirty pieces of silver!".

A less severe form of schizophrenic thought disturbance is illustrated by another patient who was writing a letter. The physician asked him to whom he was writing and what he was writing about. The patient replied, "This is a letter to my mother. The pencil I'm using has the label 'Venus Velvet 2' but the rest of the label on the pencil is scratched out except for the words 'Made in U.S.A.' The United States is a major power. I know that from what I learned in school." In this instance we see a subtle inability to organize thoughts coherently so as to give an answer to the question that the physician had asked.

Mechanisms of Defense Characteristic of Schizophrenia

Regression is the mechanism of defense which can be observed invariably in schizophrenia. The use of the mechanism of regression is responsible for many of the primitive characteristics of the patient's thought and behavior. The schizophrenic thinks in the primitive, animistic, egocentric, concrete, and omnipotent modes that characterize the small child. The return to these infantile modes of mental functioning is the result of regression.

Projection is another mechanism that is frequently used by the schizophrenic and is involved in the formation of delusions of persecution or influence and in the formation of all hallucinatory experiences.

Undoing is frequently seen in the magical gestures the schizophrenic exhibits and which he omnipotently believes can ward off evil or influence events in one way or another. Isolation of affect is involved in the calm, detached way he thinks or speaks of frightening things. He sometimes resorts to displacement with the formation of various and often bizarre phobias. He frequently uses identification, as in his delusional beliefs that he is Jesus Christ or Napoleon or some other person. He often develops strange somatic symptoms as a consequence of the use of conversion. He resorts frequently to the use of denial as he refutes the reality of events about him. In short, the profound disruption of Ego organization that occurs in the schizophrenias causes the breakthrough into awareness and behavior of all manner of primitive sexual and aggressive impulses. He frantically resorts to any and every defense mechanism available in his efforts to cope with the overwhelming flood of unconscious urges.

REFERENCES

Beck AT: Depression: Causes and Treatment. Philadelphia, University of Pennsylvania, 1967

Bleuler E: Dementia Praecox or the Group of Schizophrenias (Trans. Joseph Zinkin). New York, International Universities, 1950)

Freud S: On the grounds for detaching a particular syndrome from neurasthenia under the description "anxiety neurosis." Standard Edition, vol. 3. London, Hogarth, 1962

Goodwin FK and Bunney WE: Psychobiological aspects of stress and affective illness, in Scott JP, Senay EC (eds): Separation and Depression. Washington, D. C., Amer Assoc Adv Sci, 1973

Heinicke CM: Parental deprivation in early childhood: a predisposition to later depression, in Scott JP, Senay EC (eds): Separation and Depression. Washington, D.C., Amer Assoc Adv Sci, 1973

Kety SS: Prospects for research in schizophrenia—an overview. Neurosciences Res Prog Bull 10:456–467, 1972

Lidz T: The Origin and Treatment of Schizophrenic Disorders. New York, Basic Books, 1973

Parkes CM: Bereavement. New York, International Universities, 1972

Scott JP and Senay EC (eds): Separation and Depression. Washington D. C., Amer Assoc Adv Sci, 1973

Wender PH, Rosenthal D, Kety SS, Schulsinger F, Welner J: Crossfostering. Arch Gen Psychiat 30:121–128, 1974

6
Symptom Formation

In Chapter 4 we stated that the various mechanisms of defense can be observed in the behavior of normal people as they cope with the ordinary business of life. We emphasized that the use of defense mechanisms is not limited to the obviously pathological states of neurosis and psychosis. Some authors suggest that the term *coping mechanisms* be used to designate the defensive efforts of relatively normal people, and that we reserve the use of the term *mechanisms of defense* for the clinically abnormal. However, such usage would lead to the erroneous impression that psychopathological mental functions are fundamentally different from the psychology of the normal person. Nothing could be further from the truth. All behaviors, whether obviously abnormal or clearly normal, stem from the same sources and are governed by the same regulating principles. This is a well-documented and fundamental tenet of psychoanalysis. In this chapter we shall describe some characteristics of symptom formation and abnormal behavior, and the processes by which they arise.

FACTORS INVOLVED IN SYMPTOM FORMATION

The Concept of Primary and Secondary
Gain from Symptoms

In 1895 Freud (Breuer and Freud, 1955) discovered that psychological symptoms had meaning, performed an adaptive function, and could be understood if their underlying motivations could be discovered. Since symptoms are the product of human motivations, they represent something the patient wants and desires, even though they often are consciously experienced as painful and undesirable. In short, being the best adaptation the patient can make from the multiple forces that prompt behavior, symptoms bring the patient some advantage or gain. Psychoanalysis distinguishes between two different kinds of benefits or gains which patients derive from symptoms regardless of how distressing the symptoms may be. These are called *primary* and *secondary gain*. The term *secondary gain* is frequently used in clinical discussions. It designates some obvious advantages that accrue to the patient as a result of his symptom, such as the solicitude and sympathy that a patient with hysterical blindness may be shown by his family and friends, or the pension and discharge from the military that is granted to a soldier with crippling anxiety attacks. If secondary gain refers to benefits that accrue after symptoms have developed, what, then, is primary gain?

Primary Gain

Primary gain refers to the gain that is achieved by the lessening of anxiety through symptom formation. Primary gain motivates symptom formation. Symptoms spare the person difficult and unpleasant psychological work. For example, our patient with the phobia of thunderstorms (p. 53) was spared the difficult task of consciously confronting and resolving her rage which arose in response to being trapped in her problem-laden and dreadful marriage. She was trapped by her age, which made another marriage unlikely; by her lack of marketable skills which could support herself and her children if she divorced; by her lack of family to whom she could turn for help; and by her rigid conscience and devout Roman Catholic religious beliefs that made divorce unthinkable. Because she was trapped, her primitive, murderous rage against her husband mounted until it became terrifying and intolerable to her. If she vented it, he would surely desert her; or she might even lose control of her rage and kill him. The feared storm of rage inside her was displaced onto a suitable outside symbolic substitute—thunderstorms. This defensive displacement allowed her relative freedom from anxiety as long as the weather was good, and this compromise solution to her intense conflicts over primitive rage was the primary gain involved in the formation of her symptoms.

Secondary Gain

Secondary gain refers to the benefits that a patient derives from his illness after symptoms have developed. The phobic patient cited above illustrates this point. Once she had developed her fear of storms, she obtained much sympathy from her children, her neighbors, and her physicians, all of whom sensed the meaning and source of her terror of storms. Furthermore, she now had a potent weapon with which she could both control and punish her callous and unloving spouse. When a storm occurred, the extent of her frantic agitation forced him to come home and stay with her until the weather cleared—the only evidence of concern for her that he ever gave.

Patients do not develop symptoms to obtain secondary gain any more than a soldier arranges to have a leg shot off in war to be eligible for a government pension. Once he has lost his leg, however, he may be highly motivated to obtain as large a pension and as many other benefits as he can possibly derive from his misfortune.

Symptoms Are Compromise Formations

The formation of psychological symptoms involves a compromise between unconscious, instinctual drives which are pressing for expression and the defensive forces of the Ego which oppose those drives. Symptoms are formed when repression fails, either as a result of an increase in strength of the instinctual drives or when the organizing, controlling, and defensive functions of the Ego are weakened, enabling drives which were previously repressed and well controlled to force their way to expression. Whenever either set of conditions occurs (increased pressure of instinctual drive or decreased effectiveness of Ego function), a symptom results which reflects the attributes of both agencies involved in its formation. An example of the process of compromise in the formation of a symptom can be seen in the case alluded to in the section on conversion (p. 41). It bears repeating: A primitive murderous impulse to choke someone to death becomes too strong to be successfully defended against by repression. The mechanism of conversion is then called into play to assist in the defense. An hysterical paralysis of the hands results. The murderous urge is defended against by the paralysis which prevents the urge from actually being carried out. The hands are immobile but frozen in a clutching position such as they would assume in the act of choking someone, thus symbolically expressing the hostile urge. The patient is aware of this paralysis, but he has no awareness of the murderous intent of his anger or the symbolic meaning of the clutching position of his paralyzed hands.

Symptoms Are a Result of Impaired Ego Functions

Symptom formation occurs when the controlling and defensive functions of the Ego are no longer able to maintain successful repression, and the Ego is threatened with overwhelming anxiety associated with the eruption of primitive wishes into awareness. Additional defense mechanisms are invoked and symptoms result. The Ego may become incapable of maintaining adequate repression of instinctual drives for a variety of reasons:

1. A previously strong and well-integrated Ego may be flooded by such stressful external stimuli that Ego functioning is impaired.
2. Impaired brain function, either transient (as in toxic states) or permanent (as in senility) lessens the effectiveness of Ego operations.
3. The Ego may be *relatively* impaired by biologic factors that produce such sharp increase in intensity of instinctual drives that the Ego is incapable of maintaining adequate control over them. For example, this may occur with the upsurge of the sexual drive at puberty or at the climacteric.
4. An overly restrictive Superego that curtails even the ordinary expression of aggressive or sexual drives in day-to-day activities may interfere with effective Ego functioning. When drives are thus dammed up, they build in intensity until they break through Ego defenses, thus forcing their way into expression.
5. A weak and poorly organized Ego may maintain adequate re-

pression under ordinary circumstances even though it contains hidden defects which weaken its capacity to cope with stress. Such defects result from interferences with Ego development during infancy or childhood so that some facets of Ego function fail to proceed beyond the developmental stage at which the interference occurred. This kind of failure to move ahead is referred to as a *fixation*. Fixations create hidden defects in Ego organization which often are not apparent in the person's usual behavior, but may become manifest through the development of symptoms in situations of minimal stress and for what appears to be no obvious reason. Such a personality structure can be likened to a building which appears sturdy from the outside but contains hidden flaws in its foundation and inner structure. These flaws make it more vulnerable to the ordinary stresses that every building must be able to withstand, and it may inexplicably collapse in a storm from which other buildings survive without difficulty.

Fixation and Regression in Symptom Formation

Fixation and Its Relation to Stages of Personality Development

To clarify the concept of fixation, let us briefly examine the stages of personality development as they were initially described in 1905 by Freud (1953b) who first specified the fixed, stepwise fashion in which the psyche develops. His schema of developmental stages, organized primarily around the sexual components of behavior, are called *psychosexual stages*. In 1950 Erikson (1963) expanded on the psychoanalytic conceptualization of personality formation by examining the stages of development from the point of view of Ego functions on the one hand and social interaction on the other. His stages are called *psychosocial stages of development.* Working by entirely different means and from another theoretical framework, Piaget has described a fixed sequence of development of cognitive functions. A systematic effort to interrelate the developmental schema of Freud with those of Erikson and Piaget would take us far afield from the central task of this book. We refer the reader who is interested in pursuing the views of Erikson and Piaget to Erikson's

Childhood and Society (1963) and to the excellent resumes of the relation of Piaget's concepts to the theories of psychoanalysis by Wolff (1960) and by Elkind (1970).

Although they use different terminology and emphasize different ways of looking at psychological development, the views of Freud, Erikson, and Piaget are remarkably consistent in many of their essential features. All agree that there is a biologically fixed timetable of development, that there are definable stages of development which occur in a fixed sequence, that adult forms of behavior operate according to principles different from those by which children operate, and that the earlier and more primitive modes of psychological functioning characteristic of infants and small children are to some degree retained, reappearing in adulthood under circumstances in which regression occurs. All emphasize that biologically innate urges prompt the child to engage actively in interaction with people and things from birth onward. All agree that the people caring for the child must provide the child with stimulation adequate to his needs if the child is to develop normally.

In 1905 when Freud first coined the term *psychosexual* stage of development, he was primarily interested in the previously unexplored area of sexuality in the personality development of children. His discovery of the erotic components of behavior in infancy and childhood caused a furor in the medical and scientific community. The idea that adult sexuality had its beginnings in earliest infancy and that its manifestations could be observed throughout the various stages of childhood seemed both preposterous and immoral to many people.

He designated three stages in the first 6 years of life according to the body zone that is psychologically most important at each stage—the mouth, the anus, and the genitals. Accordingly, he labeled these three stages of development the oral stage (from birth to approximately 18 months), the anal stage (from approximately 18 months to 3 years), and the phallic (Oedipal) stage (from approximately 3 to 6 years). For reasons that we will explain, he called the period from approximately 6 to 12 years the *latency stage.*

These three body zones have obvious significance in man's sexual life. The oral zone, which figures in kissing, sucking, nibbling, and biting in ordinary adult sexuality, is the body zone through which the infant in the nursing situation has his first important emotional and physical contact with another person, usually the mother. When the mouth remains the zone that is preferred by the adult over all other body areas for sexual interchange with other persons, fellatio or cunnilingus becomes the most (or only) enjoyable sexual act. Sexually, such a person has remained in some significant degree fixated in the *oral stage.* Other psychological disturbances in adulthood which show fixation at the oral stage of development are psychogenic obesity, excessive drinking and smoking, and the schizophrenic disorders. Many aspects of the mental functions of the schizophrenic person are remarkably similar to those which psychoanalytic studies have shown to be characteristic of infants and small children. For example, schizophrenic thought is very concrete, animistic, and omnipotent, and the schizophrenic shows a marked inability to distinguish between his own thoughts and feelings and those of other people.

The growing child's struggle for autonomy and the right to assert himself center around the functions of the anal zone. Although the child clearly derives pleasure from the stimulation of this area, it also plays an important role in the expression of hostile aggression and defiance and their opposites, loving tenderness and compliance. These viscissitudes can be observed in the interplay between mother and child over issues of toilet training. In adulthood, stimulation of the anal orifice is erotically pleasurable for most people, and is a frequent part of normal sexual foreplay. The anal orifice may be the sole or preferred orifice used in homosexual or heterosexual intercourse in persons strongly fixated at the *anal stage.* The obsessive-compulsive neurosis is another disorder which involves fixation at the anal stage. Like the child at the anal stage, the person who suffers from obsessional thoughts or compulsive acts has a superstitious and childish belief in the magical power of words and gestures to control both the animate and inanimate environment. They also have great concern about their ability to exercise control over the expression of intense feelings (a psychological corollary to the child's concern with his ability to exercise control over the contents of his bowel and bladder).

In the third stage of development, the phallic-Oedipal stage, the genitals become the body zone of greatest psychological importance to the child. This stage is called the *phallic stage* because the phallus and the question of the anatomical differences between the sexes (who has a phallus and who does not) is such an important and emotionally charged issue for the child. Because children at this stage become much preoccupied with that dramatic rehearsal for adulthood, the Oedipal complex, this stage is also often called the *Oedipal stage*. The Oedipal conflict is finally resolved by repression of the aggressive fantasies of rivalry with the parent of the same sex and the erotic fantasies of intense and possessive attachment to the parent of the opposite sex. With the resolution of this conflict, early childhood ends. The *latency stage* begins.

Adults who remain fixated at the Oedipal stage tend in various respects to think and behave in ways reminiscent of the 5-year-old child. The irrational fears of the adult patient with a phobia is a clear instance, and the dramatic play-acting quality of the patient with a hysterical neurosis is another.

One can readily observe the persistence into adulthood of behaviors which result from fixations at childhood periods of development. Dedicated fingernail biters have often continued this practice since very early childhood. People who are given to phobic fears often have harbored their phobias since their Oedipal period, when many children exhibit transient phobic symptomatology. But the most dramatic instance of the profound effects in adulthood of fixation in childhood is the syndrome of the male transsexual. These patients have an intense interest in feminine activities and show marked feminine traits in their behavior from infancy onward. From the age of 2 or 3 years, most of them have shown a preference for dressing in female attire, playing with feminine toys, and pursuing characteristically feminine activities. These dramatic feminine traits are the result of the failure to resolve (that is, they remain fixated at) the level of primary identification with the mother which characterizes the infant during the first year of life.

Around the age of 6 years, children in all cultures begin instruction in the technology of their culture. It is time for the child to abandon his playlike world of make believe and fantasy in favor of the real, outside world in which he will increasingly participate. According to the studies of Freud, Erikson, and Piaget, during the period from 6 to 12 years of age the child makes major advances in personality development from the psychosexual, psychosocial, and cognitive points of view. These advances enable the child to engage in formal educational activities which prepare him for eventual entry into the world of adulthood.

Freud designated this last period of childhood, the school years before adolescence, as the latency period. The term *latency* is used in this psychosexual schema to indicate the *relative* quiescence of this stage (compared to the sexual curiosity, fantasies, and play that characterizes the prior Oedipal period) which provides an opportunity to consolidate the developmental gains of the earlier periods. This relative quiescence is soon interrupted by the resurgence of sexuality at puberty.

Freud's designation of developmental stages as psychosexual reminds us that sexual (and also aggressive) drives are of central importance to personality formation and that man begins life with no innate morality and precious little capacity to tolerate frustration, impose delay on biological urges, be guided by moral precepts, or exercise restraint and judgment. Man must, step by step, evolve from the primitive egoistic need of the child for immediate gratification of urges to the more stable, self-confident capacity of the healthy adult to tolerate frustration and give thoughtful and moral direction to his acts. To do this he must slowly develop capacities to master his own body, his wishes, and the world in which he lives. Furthermore, he must develop the capacity for mature give-and-take actions with others like him. The term psychosexual is only technical shorthand to specify certain important sexual attributes of the major way stations in this journey. In his emphasis of biological drives, Freud seemed at times to underemphasize the complexities of the social interactions between offspring and parents in the course of the child's journey to maturity. Those who are not familiar with all of Freud's writings often conclude that analysts consider the process of personality development to be primarily a struggle of the child with his instinctual urges. Although giving great weight to the biologic drives and the conflicts they cause, in 1905 Freud (1953a) recognized early the importance of ". . . the purely human and social circumstances of our patients" and commented, "Above all, our interests will be directed toward their family circumstances." It has remained for the psychoanalysts of more recent times to focus special attention on the importance of family and social factors in development.

Regression

We have used the term *regression* to designate a specific mechanism of defense, and we shall now also use it in this section to designate an integral function of the human psyche.

Each of us has a threshold for coping with stress, and if demands on the Ego become excessive, Ego functions will tend to disorganize and become ineffectual. Almost everyone has experienced episodes in his life during which many stressful events occurred in a short period of time. During such periods people characteristically make such comments as, "I have so much on my mind and feel so burdened and harassed that I can't do anything efficiently. I'm about to go out of my mind. If one more thing happens, I think I'll scream." Such descriptions indicate the sense of strain which people experience under these circumstances. Concentration, efficiency, judgment, and clarity of thought are impaired. Control over emotions is disturbed and outbursts of anger, tearfulness, or other strong feelings occur frequently. If such pressures become too intense or continue for too long a period, Ego functions will inevitably deteriorate, and the person will in some degree regress, that is, revert to modes of thought and patterns of behavior that are characteristic of earlier and less stressful periods of his life, even, at times, early childhood. Such regression is usually transient and brief, but prompt and complete recovery is possible only for people whose personality development is relatively unimpaired by traumatic life experiences during infancy and childhood. Those persons with major fixations at one or more childhood levels of development tend to regress under less stress than those who are relatively free of fixations, and to recover more slowly and less completely. Fixations produce areas of special vulnerability in the personality structure. People with such underlying fixations bear some life stresses without difficulty, but are highly vulnerable to stressful events which bear some relationship to points of fixation. Such fixations have a powerful ability to produce profound regression. As an illustration, a person whose mother died early in his life often shows a special vulnerability in adulthood to the loss of people important to him. Loss strikes at his psychological Achilles heel, whereas other stressful life events may provoke only transient distress for him.

When regression occurs, the person reverts in some degree to more childlike modes of mental function. His childlike behavior may pervade most of his activities or it may be relatively limited to some particular area of mental function. The profound regression seen in severe psychotic states often involves almost all personality functions: perception, motility, thought, and emotional expressiveness. In other instances the regression is partial and may involve only limited aspects of mental activity. For example, some people

who have mild, circumscribed, lifelong phobias function very ma-
turely in any activity which does not force them into their phobic
situation. When in the phobic situation, such people act like frightened children and often resort to childlike, magical efforts to cope
with their irrational anxiety. The woman who felt compelled to perform the ritual of buying life insurance before boarding an aircraft is
an example. Regression is inherent in symptom formation since it
always involves a retreat from the present conflict through invoking
earlier modes of mental functioning which were effective earlier in
life at their age-appropriate level.

GENERAL PRINCIPLES OF HUMAN BEHAVIOR
THAT INFLUENCE SYMPTOM FORMATION

Psychological Determinism

The data from numerous psychoanalytic researches indicate
that all behavior is psychologically determined: there are no chance
occurrences in mental life. Therefore, man does not behave in a
random or purely accidental manner. If we could sufficiently understand and correctly assess all the organizing and controlling functions of his Ego and Superego, the forces of his instinctual drives,
and the influences on him from significant people and other external
conditions in his current life, all aspects of behavior could be understood. Moreover, his behavior would prove to be the only adaptation possible for him under the prevailing circumstances. From this
view, the most complex, socially useful, and creative activity of the
scientist and the irrational beliefs and actions of the schizophrenic
person represent the only possible adaptive efforts of each person at
that moment. Society correctly evaluates the genius of an Einstein
differently than it does the irrational invention of an antigravity
device by a paranoid psychotic. But, as we shall see in a subsequent
section of this chapter, the normality or abnormality of a given
behavior cannot be decided on its social value or acceptability
alone.

The Principle of Multiple Determination

Not only is all behavior determined but also it is always determined by the multiple forces of the Ego, the Superego, the Id, and

reality. All behavior is, therefore, a compromise determined by multiple causative factors. To the degree that rational, conscious, and adult motivations predominate, the resulting behavior is normal. Normal behavior is flexible and adapted to reality; it can be changed when the demands of reality change, but it may also be continued in the face of opposition if its author chooses. However, no behavior is totally free of influences from the more infantile and irrational layers of the psyche. Freud's career as an investigator of the unconscious and infantile sexual and aggressive urges in man is a case in point. From the biographic data now available, we know that he was in some measure compelled to study such matters because of a personal need to master and resolve his own conflicts. Fortunately, this very personal motivation occurred in a person with a creative and brilliant mind. Also by good chance, he lived in a stimulating academic atmosphere at the historical moment when the psychology of man was coming within the scope of scientific investigation. His efforts, therefore, resulted in major and valuable scientific discoveries. But the fundamental forces in his personality were not qualitatively different from the forces that result in the formation of a phobia, an obsession, or a delusion.

Distinction Between Psychological Normality and Abnormality

If all behavior, whether normal or abnormal, is the product of multiple conscious and unconscious motivations, how do we differentiate between what is normal and what is abnormal? Some currently popular writers on the topic insist that neurotic or psychotic behavior is abnormal only because society has labeled it as such. This is the argument, for example, presented by members of the Gay Liberation movement who insist that homosexuality, since it is an expression of human sexuality, is in no sense abnormal, and causes no psychological suffering for the homosexual—only the moralistic disapproval of society causes this. No doubt vindictive laws and moralistic pronouncements do cause the homosexual person some distress, but neither the judgment of society nor the presence or absence of distress are valid criteria of normality or abnormality.

In our opinion, such a distinction is best made on the criteria set forth by Lawrence Kubie (1941, 1950, 1953, 1954). According to

Kubie, when infantile, unconscious, and irrational motivations predominate in the adult, his behavior will be psychologically abnormal insofar as it tends to be driven, inflexible, and unresponsive to changing social or environmental circumstances. Psychologically abnormal behavior is inflexible because the person who exhibits it is driven by unconscious needs of which he is unaware; consequently, his behavior is mostly uninfluenced by the process of rational self-evaluation or by the impact of life experience. The psychologically abnormal person therefore repeats his irrational pattern of behavior, having no capacity to modify it even when it causes suffering for himself or for others.

If such irrationally motivated and repetitious behavior happens to serve a socially valued purpose, that it is psychologically abnormal may remain obscure. The case of a respected law professor, much admired by students and rewarded by colleagues, is such an instance. Never late for a class, well prepared for lectures, and prompt in posting examination grades, he was known to all as a model of competence and reliability. Because of these characteristics, the administration relied on him heavily for assistance with difficult problems involving faculty, students, regents, legislators, and representatives of every other group or organization with problems relating to the university. Unable to refuse, or even to curtail his expenditure of time, effort, and personal investment, he eventually became overburdened and depressed and sought help.

In the course of his psychoanalytic treatment, some of the irrational and unconscious motivations that required his overly conscientious behavior became clear. Driven by an irrationally harsh and punitive Superego, the professor had no freedom to vary from his perfectionistic behavior. Like a demanding parent who insists on flawless behavior in his child, the professor's conscience allowed nothing short of absolute perfection in his work. For this reason, his holidays and weekends could not be used for relaxation, and on the few occasions that his family insisted that he go on a holiday, he was unable to enjoy the vacation because of a sense of guilt at not using his time "productively." His style of dedication to professional work was not a free choice, nor was he free to relinquish it from time to time; it was a style that he was obligated to pursue to avoid an irrational and unbearable sense of guilt and anxiety. His socially useful and acclaimed professional accomplishments were psychologically abnormal acts differing only in form and degree from an obvious compulsive symptom such as a handwashing ritual. The psychological normality or abnormality of a given behavior can be determined only by an analysis of its underlying motivations, and not by its social acceptability or unacceptability. The indices of abnormality in behavior are rigidity, inflexibility, drivenness, and insusceptibility to change in response to changing circumstances.

Definition of Psychological Illness

Psychological illness is indicated by a repetitious pattern of behavior that impairs a person's capacity for productive activity and for sustained, mutually satisfactory relations with others. The repetitious pattern itself is usually unproductive and disagreeable for the patient, and often for others in close relationship to him. It is the product of a relative predominance of unconscious and infantile sexual or aggressive drives which result in behavior that is immature and inappropriate to reality. As such, it represents a compromise formation (a "symptom") between Id and Ego, and is therefore repetitious and relatively immune to the corrective influence from ordinary life events and experience, since the rational forces of the Ego are not in command.

REVIEW OF FACTORS INVOLVED IN SYMPTOM FORMATION

Symptom formation is a complex psychological event which involves the interplay of the influences stemming from current life stress, prior fixations, the Ego and Superego, and the unconscious instinctual drives of the Id. When the controlling, organizing, and defensive functions of the Ego begin to falter, repression fails, anxiety occurs. Anxiety triggers other defense mechanisms. When they come into play, symptoms result. Symptoms develop as a compromise between the instinctual drives and the defensive efforts of the Ego. Symptoms are multiply determined and represent the only adaptation of which the patient is capable under the given circumstances. No matter how distressing a symptom may be, it is more tolerable than the amount of anxiety produced by the conflict that precipitated it. The patient's gain from symptoms is of two types: primary and secondary. His susceptibility to symptom formation depends on his general state of psychological health. The kind of symptom which he develops is a function of the defense mechanism or constellation of mechanisms that he unwittingly and automatically invokes.

CHOICE OF DEFENSE AND OF SYMPTOM

What are the factors which determine the defense mechanism (or combination of mechanisms) which a given person will use when he encounters conflict that threatens to overwhelm his Ego functions? Why does one person resort to displacement and the development of a phobia, whereas another uses isolation of affect and develops obsessional ideas, and yet a third person resorts to projection and develops delusions? Although these are reasonable questions, the answers are both complex and inadequate, and a comprehensive discussion of them would require as many more pages as we have already written and would take us far afield. We wish to note that there is no general agreement in the literature on this question and few systematic studies of it. Consequently, we shall discuss only some of the general principles which we consider to be of special significance in the determination of the choice of defense and hence also in the choice of symptoms.

The form or configuration of a symptom is mostly determined by the specific defense mechanism (or combination of mechanisms) called on to assist failing repression. If, for example, undoing is invoked, the resulting symptom will most certainly be a compulsive ritual. If, on the other hand, conversion is called into play, the symptom will inevitably be some disturbance of bodily function. But the kind of compulsive ritual and the nature of the bodily disturbance are dependent on other factors in the person's life, past and present. When a patient seeks treatment for a phobia for example, a skilled clinician can usually reconstruct the factors which caused the patient to use the defense mechanism of displacement in his attempt to resolve his conflict, but to do so requires a very detailed chronological account of that patient's life, and even the most detailed history, when obtained by the usual process of several interviews with the patient and his family, will fail to contain many of the facts that are most crucial to the understanding of the case. These deficiencies are the inevitable product of the mechanisms of defense that the patient and his family will use to protect themselves from the distress of recalling and discussing traumatic experiences which are crucial to the case. It is a common experience for psychoanalysts to learn of such crucial experiences only after a year or more of psychoanalytic sessions held four or five times weekly.

Except for Freud's famous case reports on Little Hans (1955a), the Rat Man (1955b), the Wolf Man (1955c), and Dora (1953a), few analysts have published the kind of detailed data on their patients that would be necessary to document the process of symptom formation. Indeed, the most extensive efforts by psychoanalysts to reconstruct the factors in the development of the specific defenses and symptoms of a patient are those that have been made on a case of paranoid schizophrenia in which the patient was never seen by the psychoanalysts who have written about his case. We are referring to the famous case of Schreber about whom Freud wrote in 1911 and whose case has been given further scrutiny by Niederland (1974), White (1961, 1963), and others. If the reader is interested in an account of how social, cultural, parental, occupational, and marital influences came to bear on a patient at various psychosexual and psychosocial stages of development so as to produce conflicts which led to the use of regression and projection in the formation of a schizophrenic psychosis, they can find it in these papers dealing with the Schreber case.

In the remainder of this chapter we shall deal only with those factors in the choice of defense and symptom which we regard as most important. When stress reaches a certain level, Ego functioning is impaired. Previously repressed conflictual impulses break through and are expressed in the form of compromise formations which reflect both the instinctual drive and the continued defensive efforts of the Ego. Which defense is resorted to is partly determined by the degree of regression that has occurred. When the person's personality organization regresses to the oral phase of development, he will tend to use defenses characteristic of that phase, such as denial, projection, and identification, since they are more compatible with the primitive modes of thought characteristic of infancy and very early childhood. When Ego organization regresses to the anal period, the person will use isolation of affect, undoing, and reaction formation because they are modes of mental functioning characteristic of that developmental phase. Regression to the phallic (Oedipal) phase of mental organization promotes the use of displacement and conversion, since they are characteristic modes of mental activity during the Oedipal period.

Thus we see that the depth of regression is one important factor in determining which mechanism of defense will be employed. But what determines the depth of regression? Three main factors determine the depth of the regression. One is the nature and severity of the stress that impairs Ego functioning and results in symptom formation; the second factor is the number and degree of each fixation that occurred in the patient's childhood; and the third is the point or points at which fixation occurred, that is, whether fixation took place at the oral, the anal, or the phallic stage, or to make matters more complicated, whether fixations occurred at more than one of these stages. There is much clinical evidence to support the idea that fixation at one or more childhood stages of development weakens the psychological organization of the adult. This is apparent in adults who have remained obviously fixated at childish levels of personality functioning, remaining unduly self-centered, intolerant of frustration, impulsive, and unable to exercise control over their emotions. When they encounter even mild stress, they manifest childlike helplessness and emotionality.

The interplay of these three factors can best be clarified by Freud's famous analogy regarding personality development. He likened the psyche's long developmental journey from infancy to maturity to a military campaign to take a distant objective. In such a campaign the army encounters enemy opposition along the way. At the point of such opposition, some of the troops are killed and wounded. At each such point a garrison force must be left behind to care for the wounded and cope with the enemy in that area. Thus, the strength of the army is weakened as it resumes its march toward its objective. At the next such point of opposition, more troops must be left behind to man this garrison. If too many troops have been left behind, the main force reaches its final objective in a greatly weakened condition. Then, if the enemy attacks, the troops must retreat to the nearest outpost left behind during its march. If that outpost is then attacked, a further retreat to the next outpost will be necessary, and so on.

The stress which precipitates symptom formation is, of course, relative in its effect. In people with marked fixations, slight stress provokes regression; in mature people with few and minor fixations, only extreme stress provokes regression, and when it occurs, it tends to be limited in duration, self-correcting, and less overwhelming. But of course the degree of stress which a given event imposes on a particular person also depends on the specific nature of the stress. A disturbing event, for example, the death of a loved one, tends to be more disturbing to a person who has unresolved conflicts related to important losses in childhood than it is to a person who has no such unresolved childhood conflicts. It is worth noting that the term *unresolved childhood conflict* is another way of describing a fixation.

Another factor determining a person's choice of defense and symptom is the style or characteristic mode of handling stress which prevailed in his family during his formative years. The family style is set by the parents who, in turn, reflect the style of their own parents. In families who are suspicious and blame outsiders for whatever troubles occur, projection is the predominant style. In other families who respond to stress with histrionic and dramatic headaches, vomiting, or other physical symptoms, the scene is set for the use of the defense mechanism of conversion. If the parents respond to physical symptoms in the child with great alarm and solicitude, the die is cast in favor of the victim's experiencing anxiety and hypochondriacal concerns in later life. Patients with hysterical disturbances often have shown such tendencies well back into childhood. It is unnecessary to catalog further styles of defense characteristic of specific families, but the study of Lidz (1973) which provided valuable insights into the importance of family style in inculcating the confused mode of thinking seen in schizophrenics is worthy of attention. Numerous other investigators who have studied the important field of family dynamics agree on the importance of family style in determining how children learn to interact with others, to think, to express emotions, and to cope with stress.

In addition to fixation, regression, precipitating stress, and family style, there is one other factor which we shall note only briefly: inborn temperament. It has an obvious influence on the person's style of coping with stress and a secondary influence on his preferences regarding the choice of mechanisms of defense to which he will resort. But the particular temperament of the infant is of even greater importance for the later development of psychopathology when it provokes difficulties in the mother-infant relationship. An optimally adequate mother has a wide range of ability to fit her mothering to the particular needs of her infant. Other mothers do well with infants of one temperament, but because of conflicts of their own they are unable to relate adequately to an infant of a different temperament. The case of twin adolescent girls illustrates this point. At the age of 14 one of the girls became violently abusive toward her mother and developed extreme anxiety. The other twin was well adjusted. Although they had the same mother, each had experienced a totally different style of mothering. The disturbed twin had been as active, vigorous, assertive, and strong-willed from the moment of birth as the other had been quiet, tractable, and passive. The mother, who was a somewhat rigid and controlling but kindly woman, frankly acknowledged that she had felt frustrated and angry with her disturbed daughter from the first few weeks of the child's life, whereas the needs of her passive and tractable daughter fitted the mother's style most congenially. The assertive and independent twin had been unwittingly locked in combat with her mother since birth. They never came to a mutually agreeable mode of relating with each other.

THE NEED TO RESPECT DEFENSES

Inexperienced psychotherapists tend to look on the patient's defenses as troublesome obstacles to the acquisition of insight and therapeutic change. Indeed, defenses are obstacles to therapy in that they are specifically instituted to prevent the patient from becoming aware of his own primitive impulses which he fears and wishes to disown. But if the therapist assaults defenses too hastily or otherwise inappropriately, further disruption of Ego function occurs and more profound regression comes about. The patient may then resort to more primitive and psychotic defenses.

A brief clinical example will illustrate the importance of respecting a patient's defenses and of refraining from hasty efforts to remove them, or "to break through the defenses," as some therapists say, as if they regard psychotherapy as a battle or a contest. The patient referred to earlier in this chapter who suffered from the severe phobia of storms was initially engaged in intensive psychotherapy aimed at helping her to see "the real causes" of her fear, that is, her primitive rage at her husband. In an effort to "break through her defenses," the therapist resorted to the use of amytal interviews. With the "help" of this procedure the patient suddenly realized the intensity of her hatred for her husband, but she also realized that she was unable to dissolve the marriage for the reasons noted earlier. As a result of this painful insight, she became psychotic and developed the paranoid delusion that her doctor was trying to drive her crazy and "poison her mind" with amytal. The therapist realized his error and discontinued his efforts to force the patient to acknowledge her rage at her husband. With the help of large doses of thorazine and considerable support and reassurance, the patient recovered from her paranoid psychosis. She was then treated supportively and given liberal doses of tranquilizers to lessen her terror when storms occurred. She was, after all, better off with her phobia than with any of the other options open to her.

A FINAL WORD

Given adequate knowledge of the patient and his life, we can reconstruct the process by which his symptoms came about; we can see the factors which created them and the functions they play in his struggle to come to terms with life in the only way open to him under the circumstances. The science of psychopathology has not yet achieved the precision that is possible in other branches of science. We can reconstruct how things happened much better than we can predict what will happen. As Sybil Escalona (1959) has noted, we share many of the dilemmas of the meteorologist when he attempts to predict the weather. Although we know much about the laws that govern the psyche, like the meteorologist, we deal with numerous complex variables and are often surprised by unexpected and unpredicted events. Hopefully, our understanding of the laws governing the psyche will improve as we study such unexpected and unpredicted events in the lives of our patients. In this way, we may eventually achieve the precision and accuracy of prediction that for the moment we can only admire and envy in the other branches of science. Meanwhile, we must apply what we know, and deal with our patients as best we can.

REFERENCES

Breuer J, Freud S: Studies on hysteria. Standard Edition, vol 2. London, Hogarth, 1955

Elkind D: Children and Adolescents. New York, Oxford Univ. Press, 1970

Erikson EH: Childhood and Society (ed 2). New York, Norton, 1963

Escalona S, Heider G: Prediction and Outcome. New York, Basic Books, 1959

Freud S: Fragment of an analysis of a case of hysteria. Standard Edition, vol 7. London, Hogarth, 1953a

Freud S: Three essays on the theory of sexuality. Standard Edition, vol 7. London, Hogarth, 1953b

Freud S: Analysis of a phobia in a five-year-old boy. Standard Edition, vol 10. London, Hogarth, 1955a

Freud S: Notes upon a case of obsessional neurosis. Standard Edition, vol 10. London, Hogarth, 1955b

Freud S: Psychoanalytic notes on an autobiographical account of a case of paranoia (dementia paranoides). Standard Edition, vol 12. London, Hogarth, 1958

Freud S: From the history of an infantile neurosis. Standard Edition, vol 17. London, Hogarth, 1955c

Kubie LS: The repetitive core of the neurosis. Psychoanal Q 10:23-43, 1941

Kubie LS: Practical and Theoretical Aspects of Psychoanalysis. New York, International Universities, 1950

Kubie LS: Concept of normality and neurosis, in Heiman M (ed): Psychoanalysis and Social Work. New York, International Universities, 1953

Kubie LS: The fundamental nature of the distinction between normality and neurosis. Psychoanal Q 23:167-204, 1954

Lidz T: The Origin and Treatment of Schizophrenic Disorders. New York, Basic Books, 1973

Niederland WG: The Schreber Case. New York, Quadrangle, 1974

White RB: The mother-conflict in Schreber's psychosis. Int J Psychoanal 42:55-73, 1961

White RB: The Schreber case reconsidered in the light of psychosocial concepts. Int J Psychoanal 44:213-22, 1963

Wolff PH: The developmental psychologies of Jean Piaget and psychoanalysis. Psychological Issues, monogr. 5. New York, International Universities, 1960

Index